AN
EXPANDING
FAITH

AN
EXPANDING
FAITH

by

DAVID H. C. READ

William B. Eerdmans Publishing Company
Grand Rapids, Michigan

Library of Congress Cataloging in Publication Data
Read, David Haxton Carswell.
  An expanding faith.

  1. Presbyterian Church—Sermons. 2. Sermons,
American. I. Title.
BX9178.R367E96   252'.05   73-7620
ISBN 0-8028-1539-1

To my colleagues:

William A. McQuoid
Norman D. Stanton

Preface

According to recent jargon a preached sermon may be "cool" (which is good), but a written sermon is bound to be "hot" (which is bad).

Nevertheless these sermons are submitted to the reader in the hope that the Spirit may blow upon these embers to produce the kind of temperature in which the Word may find an entrance. I trust that they will avoid the fate of that which is "neither hot nor cold" (Revelation 3:16).

Since any real sermon is born in the context of a living congregation I ask the reader to supply this background, and I salute the members of my church who thus shared in their creation. I have not tried to select "the best"—whatever that means. And since the passage of a sermon from scribble to print means hard labor for others than the author I would also salute my secretary, Carolyn Mathis, and the good people of Eerdmans Publishing Company.

David H. C. Read

Madison Avenue Presbyterian Church
New York City

Contents

1

Unloading Your Burden—
Right or Wrong?

"Bear ye one another's burdens, and so fulfill the law of Christ."

"For every man shall bear his own burden."
GALATIANS 6:2, 5

A young man has married the girl he loves. He is blissfully happy—except for one thing. Some years ago he had an affair with another girl, and he has been plagued ever since by a nagging conscience—a feeling that he treated her shabbily. That is his burden. And, during the first week of the honeymoon, he unloads it on his young wife. He tells her everything. Right or wrong?

A church member has been active in worship

and other activities for a number of years. But she becomes aware that her faith is slipping. She is no longer sure what kind of God she believes in, or what it really means to her to confess that Christ is her Lord and Savior. She develops a crushing sense of being a hypocrite when rising to sing a hymn or recite a creed. That is her burden. And one day, in a small study group with other church members, she decides to unload and tells the others all about her doubts and difficulties. Right or wrong?

The telephone rings in a private boarding school for girls. The mother of a teen-ager is calling, long distance. "Mary, something terrible has happened. Your father has left us. He wants a divorce. I just don't know what to do." That is the burden, a crushing weight she does not know how to bear. And she is unloading it on her daughter. Right or wrong?

Then, here is old man Moses—sick and tired of the nagging, murmuring, squabbling children of Israel he had led through the desert. "You are a burden," he says, "a burden too heavy for me to carry unaided. . . . How can I bear unaided the heavy burden you are to me, and put up with your complaints?" So he gets himself a council, a session of elders, and unloads. Right or wrong?

A man seems to have everything going for him—family and business flourishing, lots of friends, and bright prospects. But he has a burden. He is afraid of flying. Every time he has to make a trip by air he suffers agonies. Time and again he cancels an engagement at the last moment so that he will not have to fly. He hides his weakness as well as he can and tries everything to overcome it. Finally he goes to a psychiatrist to unload. Right or wrong?

Here is a young working woman who stayed for years with her widowed mother. The mother is what is known as a "difficult" person—querulous, inquisitive, demanding. Then she falls sick, and the daughter, after much argument and consultation, arranges for her to go to a home for old people. Right or wrong? Then let me add: the daughter is now carrying the worry about the decision. It interferes with her work, her social life, and her general happiness. So she decides to see her pastor and unload. Right or wrong?

Finally, all these people (except Moses!) are in church on Sunday morning. Into the standard words of the prayer of confession they unload all these burdens. The minister says: "If anyone is in Christ, he is a new creation; the old has passed away, behold, the new has come. The mercy of the Lord is from everlasting to everlasting. I declare unto you, in the name of Jesus Christ, we are forgiven." At that moment the loads are lifted, the burdens drop. Right or wrong?

I do not know how you are answering these questions. Probably no two of us would agree completely. I raise them to show that this matter of unloading our burdens is not as simple as preachers have often made it sound. I firmly believe that live membership in a Christian congregation should enable us to find genuine help with our burdens, that there is a sharing and an unloading to be done in the light of the gospel of Christ, and that there is something far wrong if anyone comes within range of the worship and life of any church and finds nothing to lighten the heavy load that may be pressing on him, or weighing her down. It is not much help at such a time to be prodded into action or told to "get involved." Yet there is something false in the claim that the church has a message to be applied to all your problems, a soothing ointment to be applied to all your hurts, and an immediate relief for all burdens of the heart. When Jesus invited all "that labor and are heavy laden" to come unto him, he offered rest and refreshment. "My yoke is easy," he said, "and my burden light." He did not say that there was *no* yoke and *no* burden.

This passage from Paul's letter to the Galatian church is illuminating precisely because it faces the question of our burdens with complete realism. The entire epistle reveals how deeply Paul felt his own burden as an apostle who was not only the target of a hostile world but was at times almost crushed by the misunderstandings, the pettiness, the jealousies, and the bickering within the very churches he had founded. On another occasion he refers to "the responsibility that weighs on me every day, my anxious concern for all our congregations." And Paul surely knew his Bible well enough to remember the word of the psalmist: "Cast thy burden upon the Lord, and he shall sustain thee." He tells us again and again how he was sustained, but he would have had rough words for anyone who suggested that casting our burdens on the Lord was an instant recipe for a trouble-free existence.

So, out of his own experience and that of the Galatians he was writing to, he wrote two lines that seem at first sight to be in plain contradiction but, in fact, throw the bright light of the gospel on the subject of our burdens. For him the primary question was not "How can I get rid of my own burden?" but "How can I fulfill the law of Christ—which is the law of love?" His first statement, then, is about our sharing the burdens of others.

"Bear ye one another's burdens, and so fulfill the law of Christ." Instead of concentrating on his own burdens the first duty of a Christian is to be sensitive to the burdens of others. Fulfilling the law of Christ means being prepared to accept the load from someone else rather than getting rid of our own. Really to love our neighbor is to let him unload—which means being the kind of person to whom he would naturally turn in a time of distress. That can be costly in time, energy, and inward strength. Yet it can also be a way in which mysteriously we learn to cope with our own burdens. The most overloaded, desperate people are those who can see no burden but their own. They come to believe that no one has ever had to suffer such a weight as theirs, and they become totally insensitive to the needs of others. On the other hand, the most Christian people I have known have been those who devoted themselves to a neighbor in need when their own load was overpowering. I think of a doctor I knew in Scotland giving his total attention to the troubles of a patient at a time when, as I learned afterwards, he was going through a heartbreaking domestic crisis and was himself seriously ill. I think of a minister colleague whose health was precarious and whose wife was desperately sick, who spent hours each day listening patiently and carefully to the problems of others. In today's society, where there is such temptation to harden the heart, to steel oneself against being imposed on, we need to learn again how to fulfill this law of Christ, keeping our hearts hospitable to the troubles, especially the hidden troubles, around us.

But this is more than an individual summons to be sensitive. The apostle is reminding us here of what a Christian community is meant to be. It is a *church* he is talking to. And a church is not just a place where a burdened soul can find release in prayer or in response to a sermon. It should be a place where loads can be shared in confidence and love. A large church, especially in a city, tends to offer its consolation on what one might call a one-to-one basis—in the anonymity of worship where the gospel is proclaimed, or in the private counseling of the pastors. We have to struggle to recapture the intimacy of the primitive Christian cell where a group of believers would bear one another's burdens in a pagan world. Congregations are strengthened by the growth of groups in which there can be some real sharing. No matter what brings them together—their age, a desire for prayer, a concern for housing or the drug problem, or some committee—the Spirit can move amongst us to create a sharing and caring fellowship. So my answer to all who are carrying a lonely burden, is "Yes, a church above all other communities must be a place to unload in confidence and hope."

May I add a personal word here about Moses and his problem? Do you know how much it means to a minister to feel that he does not have to carry the whole load of the church he serves? Like Moses, we have elders and deacons, officebearers. But beyond them are a host of men and women who are real burden-bearers in every possible way. This is the life of the church, where the Spirit is showing us in new ways how to "bear one another's burdens and so fulfill the law of Christ."

With this in mind—an increasing sensitivity to the burdens of others, the joy and liberation that comes from real sharing—we should find no contradiction in Paul's other word: "Every man shall bear his own burden." It is the wrong kind of sharing when we are led to hope that we can dump all our cares on someone else. Paul knew very well that, even when buoyed up by the fellowship of his Christian friends, there was always a burden that was his alone and which he could not unload on them. The law of Christ is fulfilled by those who have experienced, like Paul, not only the "power of his resurrection" but also "the fellowship of his sufferings." It is time we got rid of the false picture of the smiling family in the pew that decorates some church publications, suggesting that the ideal church is filled with carefree, untroubled people who have dumped their burdens in some celestial trash can. Every one of us here has some kind of burden that cannot be unloaded on anyone else. It is part of being a Christian. This is why, though most of us are probably too reluctant to share our troubles, we must remember that there is also a reticence that God requires, and a care for others on whom we may be shedding too heavy a load.

But this secret burden must be no secret from our God. I love the liturgical prayer that begins: "Almighty God, unto whom all hearts are open, all desires known, and from whom no secrets are hid." Do we really believe that? Or do we think that our burden is too trivial for God? Or that, on the contrary, he does not realize how heavy it is? Or that it is too sordid a matter to come into our prayers? Or that we can perhaps hide some burden from him? Or that we are required to be reticent with him?

"Cast your burden on the Lord, and he will sustain you" is not a magic formula for instant relief. It is an invitation to open our hearts completely to the Lord of life, and to experience his sustaining power. The one who sustains is not the one who entirely removed the burden. He just helps us to carry it. It is an unloading of our fears, our weariness, our self-pity—not of the burden itself. Except—except when that burden is the weight of a guilty conscience. That kind of burden no one need carry, and no Christian has a right to carry. For the gospel is the news that Christ has come to take that burden from us. The Bible portrays the guilt of us all in no uncertain terms. It is the load that in Paul's vivid phrase is around our necks like the dead prisoner to whom the live prisoner is chained: "Wretched man that I am! Who will deliver me from this body of death?" And the ringing answer comes as he remembers the one of whom it was written: "Surely he hath borne our griefs, and carried our sorrows . . . but he was wounded for our transgressions; he was bruised for our iniquities; the chastisement of our peace was upon him; and with his stripes we are healed." "Thanks be to God through Jesus Christ our Lord!" The heaviest burden ever borne by man was borne by Jesus on the cross, but from that cross he speaks the liberating word: "You are forgiven. Believe the good news; and let that burden of a guilty conscience roll down into my grave; then rise with me and live!"

There is no burden a cleansed conscience cannot bear. And there is no burden a cleansed conscience cannot understand and share.

2

When We Cease to
Be Strangers

*"Thus you are no longer aliens in a foreign land,
but fellow-citizens with God's people, members
of God's household."*

EPHESIANS 2:19

"Aliens in a foreign land." "Strangers and foreigners" says the King James Version. "Outsiders
or aliens" says J. B. Phillips. These are unpleasant
words—alien, stranger, outsider, foreigner—and
they stand for the unpleasant fact that humanity
is very far from being one big happy family. An
ugly moment for any transatlantic traveler is
when he finds himself for the first time headed
for the desk marked "Aliens." "How can *I* be an

alien?" we think, thereby confessing that for us the bulk of humanity outside our own orbit are indeed aliens—strangers and foreigners.

The concept of a stranger is perfectly natural, and you might well think that there is nothing here to talk about. No one person can possibly know more than a tiny fraction of the human race, so we need the term "stranger" to indicate all the others. No amount of prattle about the brotherhood of man can eliminate the distinction between someone you know and another about whom you know nothing whatever. We teach our children to observe this distinction. "Don't take candy from a stranger." Banks are notoriously reluctant to accept a stranger's checks.

But already, you will notice, an element of suspicion has crept in. In a perfect world even a stranger's candy and a stranger's checks would be acceptable. We could trust even the strangest stranger. As we know very well, even without the Bible's warning that this is a sinful world, a stranger may be a scoundrel even though he looks like a saint. So already the concept of stranger has an aura of suspicion and distrust. And if you have ever blundered into the wrong house or the wrong party or accosted the wrong person in the street, you know what it is like to be at the receiving end of such suspicion.

Unfortunately, we are dealing with something that goes much deeper than the natural distinction between those we know and those we do not know—something that is much more destructive than our instincts of caution. What I am talking about now was memorably illustrated in a "Punch" drawing of over a hundred years ago. Two urchins in a village street were looking at a man walking past, and the conversation went like this:

"Who's 'im, Bill?"

"A stranger!"

" 'Eave 'arf a brick at 'im."

This is what the Genesis story of the Tower of Babel symbolizes. The human race in its pretentions to grandeur falls apart. The confusion of tongues indicates the separation into "them" and "us," and the rest of the Old Testament tells us how the rival groups began heaving bricks at one another. The stranger had become, *ipso facto*, an enemy.

It is one thing to recognize that some people are strangers to us—we know almost nothing about them, their clothing, their language; their habits may be totally different from ours; and it would be absurd to pretend we were buddies. It is quite another thing to hate them for these differences, and hate can range all the way from bloody warfare to the polite social freeze. The more ingrown and cohesive a group of people, the more they tend to respond to the foreigner by heaving a brick.

The world that Jesus knew was filled with strangers. The Romans were strangers to the Jews;

the Jews to the Samaritans; the Pharisees to the Sadducees; the Zealots to the police; the poor to the rich. There in one little stretch of territory about the size of Connecticut was concentrated a volume of stranger-hating like that which poisons our world today. And it was there that a movement began to take the sting out of the word "stranger," to defuse the passions that animate one group of human beings against another, and to create a world where no one is ever a total stranger to others or to God.

Jesus was thoroughly a man of his time and race. He was every inch a Jew in training, loyalties, and habits of thought and speech. He completely accepted the local boundaries of his mission, and there is no evidence that he had ambitions to roam the ancient world as a rootless preacher and teacher to all the nations. He lived in an atmosphere where the concept of "stranger and foreigner" was rigidly applied to every Gentile, and where even among the Jews there were fixed barriers between the inner circle of the "righteous" and the mass of "sinners." Yet Jesus broke clear through these barriers by his total refusal to treat anyone as a stranger with whom he could have no dealings. The moment anyone came in contact with him he or she was no longer a stranger. They were in the presence of one who saw them as human beings and was ready to respond to their needs. He talked about the Kingdom of God as a festival to which everyone was invited and where no one was a stranger. "From east and west people will come, from north and south, for the feast in the kingdom of God." Have you noticed how the stranger is often the hero of the stories he told—the stranger who refuses to be a stranger? The Samaritan was the one person on that Jericho road who might well have hurried past the wounded Jew as a stranger and foreigner, but he was the one who stopped. Those who are to be welcomed at the right hand of the Father in glory, he said, are the ones who helped those they did not know. And they would make the discovery that the Lord himself was present in the stranger. "For when I was hungry, you gave me food; when thirsty, you gave me drink; when I was a stranger you took me into your home, when naked you clothed me; when I was ill you came to my help, when in prison you visited me."

Now we begin to see that Jesus did more than merely declare that no one is a stranger because "he is not one of us." As the story unfolds we see him more and more accepting the role of the stranger himself. Part of what is meant by his redemptive passion, "bearing our griefs and carrying our sorrows," is just this willingness to go through the agony of the one rejected by every human society, not only the foreigners who ruled the land but his own people, and not only by their leaders but finally by his own most intimate friends, and even, in one terrible moment on the cross, the agony of one rejected by his God. It is the world's most utter stranger who hangs there at Calvary. He lets the weight of the rejection, fear, and hatred that have poisoned the word stranger on human lips fall on him. And in that sacrificial moment he extracted the sting and made possible a new humanity where no one is a stranger to be rejected, but all are at home in the Father's house.

That this was not a fantasy dreamed up by the friends of Jesus who claimed to have seen him alive again is demonstrated by what happened when the church was launched on its mission to the world. At Pentecost the Spirit broke loose to reverse the demonic divisions and factions of the Tower of Babel. The gift of tongues symbolized a new power of communication across the barriers and a new sense that where the Spirit of Christ is, there can be no strangers. That day the church threw open its doors to everyone within reach and went on to bring to the entire world the story of the Stranger who died so that every man and woman could find a home and a welcome in the Kingdom of God. Within a few years of Pentecost, Paul, a Pharisee of the Pharisees, could be writing to the Gentiles at Ephesus: "You are no longer aliens in a foreign land, but fellow-citizens with God's people, members of God's household."

I believe that at this point in the long history of the church the Spirit is moving us again to be the healing and reconciling community where no one is treated as a stranger. The sad history of Christian exclusiveness with its freeze on human contacts with other faiths and its spawning of dozens of denominations, who look on one another as strangers, has to be reversed. Without in any way abandoning our loyalty to Christ as the Lord and Savior, we can seek and find our common humanity and resist the diabolic temptation to see any race or class of our fellow-creatures as strangers—and, therefore, targets for our bricks. How much effort do we make really to know strangers, people of different ethnic or religious backgrounds from our own? How much have we done to respond to the inarticulate cry of the lonely ones who live nearby yet find no place where they do not feel total strangers?

I do not want to leave some vague impression of the church as a reconciling force in our divided world. The Bible does not deal in generalizations. It is always factual, concrete, and personal. The tremendous story of God's love for us in Christ is not left in the clouds. As he came in the flesh and blood of a Palestinian Jew so he comes in the visible, tangible bread and wine of communion. As he took that bread and said, "This is my Body," so he also takes *us*, the community of his followers, and says, "This, too, is my Body." And the word he speaks through this body is still: "You are no longer aliens in a foreign land, but fellow citizens with God's people, members of God's household."

Among the many things we know we have to do as the Body of Christ where he has placed us, one we should never forget. We must cease to be strangers. And that does not happen by an announcement from the pulpit. It happens as each member comes alive to the power of the one who let himself be made a total stranger so that no human being should be excluded from the family of God. Then it will be recognized that the church is no club that looks on its neighbors as strangers and foreigners, but a living cell of the Body of Christ on earth, as open as he was to the needs of all around and as receptive to their unique qualities in the family of mankind. There should be nothing in the common life or worship of a church that would make anyone at all feel like an alien in a foreign land, not "our kind of people."

At the center stands the symbol of the cross on which the Stranger died. It is empty, for he is now the one who is no stranger anywhere. It is his invitation that comes to all who enter. "Come unto me and I will give you rest"—rest from that alienation of spirit, that sense of being a stranger before God and man. The Table makes this house a home, a home where the welcome sign is out for all who seek communion with this Lord and those who are in any sense going his way. Our Savior invites those who trust him to share the feast he has prepared. Where Christ is alive and active in the sacrament of the bread and wine and meets us simply as human beings in our common need is where we cease to be strangers. The one with whom you receive the elements of Holy Communion is your sister or brother in Christ.

3

Love—When We Are Angry?

"If you are angry, do not let anger lead you into sin; do not let sunset find you still nursing it; leave no loophole for the devil. . . . Have done with spite and passion, all angry shouting and cursing, and bad feeling of every kind."
EPHESIANS 4:26, 27, 31

Christians are supposed to follow the way of love. We are to love other people in all circumstances, no matter who they are, even if they count themselves our enemies. Jesus said that love was the great commandment—love for God and love for our neighbors. Paul ranked love as the supreme Christian quality, above even faith and hope. And love is spelled out for us in practical terms—helping, forgiving, caring, seeking the other person's good. It is to this kind of life, to this attitude to those who cross our path, that we are committed—no matter how far short of it we fall. This passage from Ephesians drives it home again: "Be generous to one another, tender-hearted, forgiving one another as God in Christ forgave you." We can have no doubt about this being the one dominating, absolute principle for the Christian. At all times, and with all people without exception, act in love.

Then how about your anger?

Perhaps you wish to argue that you have no anger, that you are so possessed by the Spirit of Christ that you have eradicated all anger from your heart. It may well be that you have learned not to explode, that it has been years since you blew your top. Perhaps you can sincerely say that there is no one you hate, no one to whom you wish any kind of ill. But give a good psychiatrist half a chance, and he will almost certainly uncover a smoldering volcano of rage and anger you did not know was there. He may even suggest that sitting on that volcano is a reason for the moods of depression that afflict you—a suggestion that might touch off some of the rage you have been hiding! However, as Jesus said, "you shall know the truth, and the truth will set you free." And the truth is that we are all at times very angry men and women. If we were not, we should be scarcely human. (In that very human book we call the Old Testament, one little word meaning "anger" occurs **224** times. This word, even if it applies at times to God himself, is no mild term: it literally means "snorting.")

If anger, then, is rooted in our humanity, the question arises as to whether it belongs to what Paul calls the "old man," the sinful nature that has to be replaced by the new "man in Christ." To put it another way: is anger ever compatible with love? Can you think of no time when the anger of a parent, a teacher, a friend—or a politician or a preacher—seemed to you perfectly wholesome and Christian? Are we right to assume that anger is the opposite of love? Hate, yes: hatred has no place in a life dedicated to love. But anger?

What does the Bible say? This passage from Ephesians has more to say about anger, and with more fascinating implications, than any other I know. It is all the more helpful for us in that it was written by the hot-blooded and irascible apostle who was not known to suffer either fools or knaves gladly. I sometimes wonder if his bad temper was not the "thorn in the flesh" he prayed to have removed. The contrast between Paul and his Master at this point is highlighted by their behavior when each in turn appeared before the ecclesiastical court. Here is Jesus: "At this the High Priest rose and said to him, 'Have you no answer to the charge that these witnesses bring against you?' But Jesus kept silence. . . . Then they spat in his face, and struck him with their

32

fists." And here is Paul: "At this the High Priest Ananias ordered his attendants to strike him on the mouth. Paul retorted, 'God will strike you, you whitewashed wall!' "

So it is from a man of fiery temperament that we hear the Word of God on the subject of anger. And you will find that there is no contradiction between what he has to say and the Spirit of the Lord who inspires him.

His first words on the subject are startling. "If you are angry, do not let your anger lead you into sin." At once we learn that anger is not necessarily sin. "If you are angry"—he accepts the possibility without condemnation. In fact, the Greek is much more explicit. It is an imperative, which the King James Version retains: "Be angry, and sin not." Whatever Paul meant—the extraordinary commandment: "Be angry" or just "If you are angry"—we are clearly being told that a Christian can be angry without betraying the rule of love.

Lest we should think that Paul is here giving us an "out," saying in effect that, after all, we cannot be expected to love all the time, or making allowance for his own temptations to blow off steam, we should have another look at the Gospel record of Jesus in action.

The word "anger" is not common in the Gospels, but on at least one occasion it is bluntly applied to the reaction of Jesus to the people around him. In a synagogue that he was attending one Sabbath there was a man with a withered arm. Immediately the love that was in him went out to the sufferer. And immediately his critics seized on the occasion to accuse him of being a Sabbath-breaker. As he called the man out before him he posed the simple question: "Is it permitted to do good or to do evil on the Sabbath, to save or to kill?" Then we read: "They had nothing to say; and, looking round at them with *anger* and sorrow at their obstinate stupidity, he said to the man, 'Stretch out your arm.' " It was the sheer inhumanity of these so-called religious people that incensed him. Sorrow, yes; but also anger. The Lord of love was clearly capable of a blazing anger—an anger without sin.

This is not an isolated incident in which Mark has perhaps chosen an unfortunate word. (It is interesting that Matthew and Luke, following Mark closely here, deliberately omit this word that bothered them.) If we read the Gospels without any preconceptions about a "gentle Jesus, meek and mild" we shall find that time and again his anger flared—against inhumanity, yes, and also against hypocrisy, against the demonic powers, against all who offended children, and against the diseases that he saw crippling God's children. He lashed out at the cities that refused the summons to conversion, and at the traffickers who profaned the Temple. All this in spite of his constant compassion and longing for the salvation—the physical, mental, and spiritual health—of everyone he met. You cannot study the whole picture of Jesus without realizing that there is such a thing as the anger of love.

And is this not what to some degree his disciples must reflect in every age? Is it possible to love in the spirit of Jesus without being at times moved to anger? There is something wrong with a love for our neighbors that never feels anger when they suffer from neglect, oppression, inhumanity, or injustice. Do you not think that some of us should be more angry than we are about some of the things we have learned to live with in this country—rat-infested slums, overcrowded courts and prisons, the traffic in narcotics, and the attitude of "Let's not get involved"? The trouble is that, while Jesus raged against the forces in his day that despised the weak and enslaved the bodies and souls of human beings and damaged little children, our anger seldom mounts until we ourselves are touched and our own security is threatened.

Christian anger should be aroused by all that hurts our neighbor and not just touched off when, for instance, we ourselves become the victims of "crime in the street." This is hard, for it takes an immense dose of sympathy and imagination to put ourselves in the shoes of other victims of violence and oppression when we are untouched. And there is nothing like personal injury for arousing our rage. Yet, we must thank God for the Christian anger of those in the past who have raged against slavery, injustice, and brutality, and for those today who will not let our conscience be at rest while any of our neighbors suffer.

"Be angry, and sin not." "If you are angry, do not let your anger lead you into sin." One more translation—J. B. Phillips—"If you are angry be sure that it is not out of wounded pride or bad temper." These words remind us that what is called "righteous wrath" is a dangerous and delicate concept. I have tried to sketch what it means, but the Bible warns us how justified anger about evil conditions can be twisted into self-serving explosions of temper or expressions of our own aggressiveness and pride. I have pointed out how quick we are to express our rage when such conditions begin to touch us personally, but it is equally possible for an anger against some social evil to be an excuse for a spirit of constant irritability, touchiness, and aggression.

So Paul goes on: "Let not the sun go down upon your wrath." "Do not let the sunset find you still nursing it." And he adds "Leave no loophole for the devil." An outburst of anger, no matter how justified, offers some wonderful loopholes for the devil—the devil of indulging in smoldering rage, for instance, or the devil of nursing a grudge, or the devil of actually enjoying our righteous indignation. We have to ask ourselves just one question to see what he means. Can you imagine Jesus, on the day he exploded against the hard-hearted legalists in the synagogue, brooding all day on the incident, going to bed consumed with ugly thoughts about his enemies and waking the next day obsessed by this incident? To have his spirit is to know the virtue of a bright, clean rage against inhumanity and hardness of heart that is never perverted into a lingering poison that corrupts the soul. Too well do we know what Burns meant when he described Tam O'Shanter's wife as "nursing her wrath to keep it warm."

Never has it been more urgent for the forces of goodwill in this country to make this distinction between a salutary anger and the aggressiveness that sparks into unbridled rage. We need the wrath of love to keep us from tame acquiescence in evil conditions. But also we need desperately to be delivered from the mounting anger that springs from fear and prejudice, from racial and religious antagonisms, from the hatreds that are smoldering in the hidden depths of our society. This is the anger that can tear a society apart. This is the anger that is exploding into acts of savagery, murder, and open war in a world that is supposed to have "come of age." This kind of anger escalates demonically as one atrocity breeds another, and even the mildest people become blinded by the climate of hate. It grows by what it feeds on—and what it feeds on is listed in this passage of Scripture. "Have done with spite and passion, all angry shouting and cursing, and bad feeling of every kind."

If we are to avoid catastrophe, there must be a

radical defusing of the spite and passion, the angry shouting and cursing, the bad feeling which threatens us all. And that is the task of churches and synagogues—not only to prod the conscience of the comfortable, to rouse clean anger against inhumanity and oppression, but to create a climate of calm, to moderate the language of polemic, to break down racial and ethnic barriers that keep us from knowing one another as human beings, and to extirpate the bad feelings we may nourish against those with whom we disagree. There is altogether too much rage seething in the world today, and now is the time both to tackle its causes and to set a watch on our lips.

Love—when we are angry? Yes, love is the only power that can channel anger in the right direction and prevent it exploding in acts of bitterness and hate. The apostle ends with the Christian way of love, and in his final words reveals its motive power. "Be generous to one another," he says, "tender-hearted, forgiving one another. . . ." Generosity, compassion, and the forgiving spirit. Where can we find the inner resources for such a program? Only, we are told, as we see ourselves as we really are—not paragons of virtue who are the victims of wicked people and evil systems, but as guilty sinners who have been accepted and are constantly forgiven through the grace of God. "Forgiving one another," he says, "as God in Christ forgave you." Anyone who really believes that he or she is freely forgiven, accepted in

Christ, has the starting place for a campaign of generosity, compassion and forgiveness in dealing with others whoever they may be. It is Christ himself who can burn the hatred out of our hearts as we go to battle against the evil things in our society today.

4

New Life in Our Prayers

"Lord, teach us to pray . . . "

LUKE 11:1

At first sight this is an odd request. "Lord, teach us to pray." These were people who had almost certainly been praying all their lives. As practicing Jews they would have been taught to pray as soon as they could speak, and probably not a day passed without some form of prayer. Why should they suddenly say "Teach us to pray"?

Let me change the subject. I have been playing golf ever since I was six years old—recently about once every five years. Suppose I were suddenly to find myself marooned on an island with a beautiful course and nobody to play with except Jack

Nicklaus. If I had watched him in action, might it not be perfectly reasonable for me to say: "Jack, teach me to play"? Extend the thought in any direction you like—from cooking to playing the piano. Is it not true that something one has done for years looks very different when one is in the presence of an expert, a master of the art? In their presence one feels like beginning all over again. So it undoubtedly was for the disciples when they had lived with Jesus. Here was a master of prayer, and in his presence they felt they knew almost nothing about it.

I am addressing here people who pray, not only in church but alone. Some of us might confess to the merest fragment of prayer life; some may find it a daily joy and necessity; nearly all of us have memories, at least, of the prayers we were taught as children. So I am not speaking to the persons Job described so eloquently—the happy heathens who are perfectly satisfied with their prosperity, who never had it so good, and have no need of God.

> Their seed is established in their sight with them, and their offspring before their eyes. Their houses are safe from fear, neither is the rod of God upon them. Their bull gendereth, and faileth not; their cow calveth, and casteth not her calf. They send forth their little ones like a flock, and their children dance. They take timbrel and harp, and rejoice at the

sound of the organ. They spend their days in wealth, and in a moment go down to the grave.

We do not need much imagination to transpose the terms and to recognize the fat cat for whom everything goes well. He has a large and healthy family. No illness or accident seems to hit him. He finds his bulls in the stockmarket, sends the children to luxury camps, and has a beautiful stereo in his duplex. And he rounds it off with a quick and painless death. This is the man who needs no religion and who never prays. "What is the Almighty that we should serve him? and what profit should we have if we pray unto him?"

If that were your attitude, you probably would not be reading this book. Still, you may perhaps be at times inclined to share Job's complaint. He is answering the smooth theories of his religious friends who assure him that the man who honors God will be successful while the ungodly will come to grief. "Not at all," says Job. "I've seen lots of the ungodly who sail through life with everything they want, and here am I, who always said my prayers, with my life in ruins about me and covered in boils." Is this not what makes us sometimes wonder about prayer—the blunt fact that people who do not pray often seem to get along famously, while we have gone through little hells without, it seems, an answer to our prayers. If this *is* your question, do not despair. It is far better to raise it, like Job, than to pretend that prayer is a simple exercise with obvious results. I would rather learn about prayer from Job than from his comforters. This man won through. And I would rather learn about prayer from Jesus than from the modern comforters who assure us it will bring material success. For his prayer life culminated in a crucifixion, a crucifixion that he prayed with sweat and blood might not happen. And he won through. So, with even greater urgency and confidence than his disciples, who had not yet seen where he was going, we must want to plead: "Lord, teach us to pray."

I urge you to join me in that prayer for two reasons. First, I am confident that we all, in varying degrees, feel the need for new life in our prayers. How vitally are we engaged in the prayers we make together? Is something really happening when we confess our sins and pray for God's gifts for ourselves and other people? If you said a prayer by yourself on rising this morning, was it joyful, energetic, heartfelt, and alive? Have prayers become a duty that lies heavy on your conscience, or are they a stimulation and a delight? Most of us know those moments when we could paraphrase Hamlet and say, "How weary, stale, flat, and unprofitable seem to me all the uses of these prayers."

Second, I believe that Jesus can teach us to pray—whatever stage we are at. Just as he clearly

43

transformed the prayers of these disciples who were already praying people, he can refresh and renew our prayers today. In fact, he begins to do so the moment we listen to him, for he invites us to live in his Father's world, which is a world of mystery, of expectation, and endless horizons, so different from the constricted world of modern secularism with its stifling atmosphere of statistics, projections, and manipulation of the human spirit. If, like me, you increasingly resent a world where the unexpected cannot happen, where everything from making love to composing a sonata is scientifically explained and technologically controlled, where some computer already knows how we are going to vote and how long it will be before the human race starves or suffocates, then you are ready to learn again from Jesus about that larger world in which our wills and the will of the living God are still alive and active. As a Scottish theologian I knew used to say: "The universe is not an iron gauntlet in the hands of God: it is a velvet glove." It is such a universe—of infinite pliability, flexibility, and possibility—that Jesus offers us and will guide us into. The point of entry is our prayers.

In answer to the disciples' request Jesus did two things. First, he offered a model, a prayer they could all learn and use. Then he offered, as he did at other times, some startling images to make his disciples rethink their ideas about the God to whom they were praying. In speaking about new life for our prayers today, I want to confine myself to these two ways of refreshment.

Perhaps you will say: What is so refreshing about model prayers? Is it not this business of rattling off set formulas that makes prayer automatic, mindless, and unreal? I remember once feeling this so strongly that I believed the church had made a mistake in formalizing the repetition of the Lord's Prayer, which was no more than a suggestion. When a friend of mine with similar ideas asked one of our professors if he would *have* to repeat the Lord's Prayer in every Sunday service, he was told: "Not if you know a better." That made me reconsider.

I believe now that our Lord did offer a set piece for our prayers. It was the custom of contemporary rabbis and teachers to do so, and it is probably true that Jesus himself used set prayers in his own communion with his Father. I do not mean that he used *only* this kind of prayer or expects us to do the same. On the contrary, he talked about going into a little room alone and talking to God as naturally as a child to a father. That must have been happening also on those nights when he spent hours alone on the hilltops in prayer. But he knew the value of the remembered prayer, the prayer that linked him with his own spiritual past and with the great community of believers on earth and in heaven. The prayers he used in the terrible moments of Gethsemane and Calvary were surely remembered prayers, familiar prayers, prayers he knew by heart. "Let this cup pass from my lips"; "Not my will but thine be done"; "Father, forgive them, for they know not what they do"; "Father, into thy hands I commend my spirit." This last was probably the last thing he said every night on going to sleep.

The value of such learned prayers lies in their accessibility at such moments of stress and even despair when it is not easy to pray. It also lies in their power to link us to that wider world of which I spoke. We should not be too much troubled by the fact that often we seem to repeat the words without really thinking what we are saying. Provided we do not think that there is virtue in merely rattling off a form of words, we can find in them an avenue to God—even when our attention is relaxed. But their renewing power lies in the fact that a prayer which has stood the test of time can at any moment spring to life and transform our relationship to God and other people. Edwin Muir, who is probably the most distinguished Scottish writer of this century and is one of those modern intellectuals who, like C. S. Lewis, found their way from agnosticism to full Christian belief, vividly describes the moment when he suddenly found himself repeating the Lord's Prayer "with deep urgency and profound emotion." "Every word had a strange fulness of meaning which astonished and delighted me . . . meaning after meaning sprang from it, overcoming me with joyful surprise; and I realized that this simple petition was always universal and always inexhaustible and day by day sanctified human life."

The use of such prayers can have just this effect of sanctifying human life, provided we keep alive to the energy of the Holy Spirit. New life can come to our prayers as we make use of these links with the eternal. There are hundreds available from the beautiful collects of the church universal to the "arrow prayers" that many are finding helpful in our days of stress and bustle. An arrow prayer is a short petition winged to God at a moment's notice. "Thank you, Lord." "Guide me, O God." "Bless the Lord, O my soul." "Lord, I believe; help thou mine unbelief." "Speak the word only and thy servant shall be healed." J. D. Salinger's novel *Franny and Zooey* popularized in some quarters an ancient prayer of the Eastern church: "Lord Jesus Christ, Son of God, have mercy on me." Some have abbreviated this prayer to the single word "Jesus" (better not said aloud in case you are misunderstood!), and, provided we avoid a feeling of magic in the name, it can be a salutary habit.

The "arrow prayer" is a natural expression of our constant dependence upon God. There is a good example of one in the Bible story of Nehemiah, who was a Jewish courtier in the palace of the Persian emperor. Like many exiled Jews in every generation he longed to return to Jerusalem and made up his mind to make such a request. His opportunity came when the king one day remarked on his sad countenance. "Then I was sore afraid, and said to the king, let the king live for ever: why should not my countenance be sad, when the city, the place of my fathers' sepulchres, lieth waste, and the gates thereof are consumed with fire? The king said unto me, For what dost thou make request? *So I prayed to the God of heaven,* and I said to the king. . . ." There is real life in our prayers when it becomes natural for us to send up an SOS at such a moment!

There is much more to be said about the renewal of prayer through the lively use of such forms—and also through the use of gestures, objects, symbols, and body movements. In an age of so much nonverbal communication we should not allow ourselves to be hung up by our historic prejudices but should feel free to use whatever familiar gesture expresses our penitence or praise or desire to invoke God's blessing on another. All these things are linking us daily and practically to that dimension where, as Jesus says, "all things are possible to those who believe."

Now we turn to the second aspect of the renewal of our prayers. I am thinking about the image of God and of our relationship to him. After all, without some sense of God's reality and presence, prayer becomes just talking to ourselves or others—which is what many current prayers tend to be. The stronger our conviction about God, the more life there will be in our prayers.

What strikes me about the stories Jesus told about prayer is that they are always unexpected, sometimes funny, and occasionally almost shocking. It is unexpected to be reminded that we are slow to believe that God would be as ready to give us good things as we are to our children. It is funny to be told about the man who woke his neighbor in the middle of the night to borrow bread, and would not go away. And it is shocking to be told about the judge who gave in to a widow's petition simply because she kept pestering him—shocking, that is, if we think Jesus is saying that God is just like that. I believe we have to take each of these tales and let them speak. The point is that our Lord is shaking up a lot of conventional beliefs. He is asking us to think again about God and how he deals with our prayers, and about our own indolence in asking.

This is a huge area where there is still much to be discovered. But let me make one suggestion. It has to do with what, for want of a better expression, we call "the God above us" and "the God within us" (if you like—"God transcendent" and "God immanent"). I am not one who believes that we are mistaken in holding to the belief in the God whom the prophet beheld "high and lifted up," when he heard the angelic chorus: "Holy, holy, holy is the Lord of hosts: the whole earth is filled with his glory." Now more than ever, that note needs to be sounded in our worship and devotional life. But is it not true that most of us tend rather exclusively to think of the God we speak to in prayer as one who hovers "out there" waiting to hear from us? It is hardly too much to say that he is the God whose number we ring together in church on Sundays or in emergencies during the week. I am convinced that the living God is personal, but surely not in the sense that he is *a* Person to be located some distance away.

Our prayers might take new life if we opened our minds and hearts to the equally biblical concept of "the God within us," the God who is to be found *in* the daily duties, *in* our encounters with one another, *in* the beauty of his universe, *in* the voice of the arts and sciences, and *in* the very center of our own being. The Bible uses special images as it speaks of "calling upon the Lord," or "lifting up our prayers to him," but it also tells us of the God within who hears before we ask, of the voice that echoes in our own souls. In the Pentateuch the word of the Lord is not just that which thunders from Sinai. "The word is very nigh unto thee," says Deuteronomy, "in thy mouth, in thy heart." The prophets were overwhelmed by the transcendent glory of God, but they could write of his nearness and intimacy. "After these days, saith the Lord, I will put my law in their inward parts, and write it in their hearts; and will be their God, and they shall be my people," says Jeremiah. And Isaiah hears the words: "I dwell in the high and holy place, with him also that is of a contrite and humble spirit, to revive the spirit of the humble, and to revive the heart of the contrite ones."

It is this sense of "the God within" that springs to life in the New Testament teaching about the Holy Spirit. Can you read the last chapters of John or the epistles of Paul with this in mind without realizing the tremendously reviving power of the inward presence of God's Spirit? What could it not do for our prayers to realize in a new way that God is not a distant being waiting for our call, but the one within moving us and the whole human family towards the Kingdom of his Christ? It is one thing to put through a long distance call to a wise friend in a time of trouble: it is quite another to commune inwardly with such a friend and be aware of such an influence and such a love. This new life in our prayers demands more than an effort of the mind to pry open old concepts and images. It means learning to be quiet, learning to meditate, and knowing that, before we even begin to pray, God is already there.

5

What Makes
You Think of God?

"Hear, O Israel, the Lord is our God, one Lord, and you must love the Lord your God with all your heart and soul and strength. These commandments which I give you this day are to be kept in your heart; you shall repeat them to your sons, and speak of them indoors and out of doors, when you lie down and when you rise. Bind them as a sign on the hand and wear them as a phylactery on the forehead; write them up on the doorposts of your houses and on your gates."

DEUTERONOMY 6:4-9

During summer vacations, living as a layman always teaches me something.

By "living as a layman" I mean not having any sermon deadline to drive me to my Bible, not having to offer prayer in church or homes or hospitals or at public functions, mixing with people in trains and buses and cafes who have no idea I am a clergyman, and waking up in the morning without wondering how I can write that review of a theological book today when there are two TV shows to be taped, four interviews, a wedding rehearsal, and a session meeting. I am not suggesting that my working life is any fuller than anyone else's, but that it naturally concerns what we call religion. It forces me to think about God. And living as a layman for a while shows me how easy it must be to get along without much conscious thought about God at all. For we are living in a society where there is not much to remind us of the divine, very few signs or symbols in daily life that compel us to think about God.

It was very different in biblical times. It was very different in the Middle Ages. It may even have been different for some readers who can remember a childhood when there were family prayers, a community where the church was central, and a Sunday where there was a curious spiritual hush. From the Old Testament we know that the people of Israel were surrounded by signs of God's presence. From the Temple in Jerusalem to the most distant village there were shrines, tombs, holy places, and ceremonies designed to remind the Israelite of the living God and his concern for his people. Every aspect of daily life was sanctified in prayer and ritual so that no child could possibly grow up in ignorance of the divine presence. Similarly, in the Middle Ages the Catholic Church covered human life from the cradle to the grave with her sacraments and ceremonies, and the parish church or cathedral brooded over the community like a hen over her chicks. Every painter, architect, writer, and musician seemed driven to express glory to God—or at least to choose religious themes in which to express his genius. Even after the Reformation had broken this total dominion of the Roman Church and swept away many of the signs and symbols the Protestant nations still clung to the notion of a Christian country and developed a piety and polity that was calculated to remind every citizen of the presence and demands of God from birth to death.

Recent travels have taken me not only through the USA and Canada, but also to Russia, England, Scotland, and France. And there is certainly less difference today between any of these lands as typical modern secular societies than between any one of them now and the same land a hundred years ago. In any one of them you might almost say that a hundred years ago it took a lot of nerve and strength of will to be an atheist while today it takes a lot of nerve and strength of will to be a believer.

What in your daily round helps to make you think of God?

From a land that has emphasized the separation of church and state, you might expect a secular world that offers little or nothing to remind one of the transcendent. But we have now reached a point where the churches themselves have been busy removing the signs and symbols of the eternal and invisible. Malcolm Muggeridge, writing recently in the London *Times*, says:

> In this modernizing process, whether in the most august Roman Catholic congregations or the most wayward and obscure of little Bethels, the same principle would seem to be at work—to make worship as like as possible to everyday life, in its language, its exhortations, its music, and its petitions. Whereas the great cathedrals and other monuments to Christendom's two thousand years were designed to express the awe, wonder and joy of men audaciously reaching up to God, and the corresponding thankfulness that God should have deigned to become incarnate and reach down to them, the present tendency is, as it were, to look God straight in the eye and address him accordingly.

I sympathize with Mr. Muggeridge's criticism of the secularization of the church. Yet, at the same time, we must not idealize the past and imagine that the people of the Bible or of the Middle Ages were by nature and practice necessarily more gen-

uinely devout than contemporary Christians and
Jews. The evidence is that both the Israelites and
the inhabitants of Christendom needed constant
prodding to remember their God and to obey his
laws. This is exactly what is expressed in the
central passage from the Pentateuch cited above:
"These commandments which I give you this day
are to be kept in your heart; you shall repeat
them to your sons, and speak of them indoors
and out of doors, when you lie down and when
you rise. Bind them as a sign on the hand and
wear them as a phylactery on the forehead. . . ."
In these verses we find the three elements that are
needed in every generation for the creation and
maintaining of a lively sense of the reality and
presence of the living God.

Judaism and Christianity are agreed on this as
the central obligation of every man or woman.
"The Lord is our God, one Lord, and you must
love the Lord your God with all your heart and
soul and strength." That is the Shema of the
synagogue to this day—"Hear, O Israel." And the
writers of the Westminster Catechism said the
same thing when they wrote the answer to the
first question: "The chief end of man is to glorify
God and to enjoy him for ever." It is all very well
to have such resounding statements about our
duty to God, but whether we live in ancient
Israel, seventeenth-century Scotland, or twenti-
eth-century America, they can be mere religious
rhetoric suspended in the stratosphere while we

go about our business without one serious thought of God.

So the word is added: "These commandments which I give you this day are to be kept in your heart." *In your heart.* Knowledge of God, belief in his reality, desire to serve him are to be nourished in the very depth of our being. *In your heart.* The evidence of God is not primarily in the world of his creation, or the story of humanity, or the compulsions of conscience, but in the secret place where the self is formed, where we come to know who we are and to whom we belong. Thinking about God should not be an effort of the mind whereby we force ourselves to accept some religious doctrine. It should be the natural flowering of an inward communion. A man in love does not force himself to think about his beloved. It happens constantly simply because she is in his heart. Just because the Bible, especially in the Old Testament, talks so much about law we must not imagine that our relationship to God is a matter of following certain rules and training the mind to believe and obey. Throughout the Bible it is the heart we hear about, the inward delight in God, the warmth and spontaneity of true communion with him. "Thy word have I hid in my heart," cries the psalmist. "Keep thy heart with all diligence," says the proverb, "for out of it are the issues of life."

It was this inner direction and affection of the heart that Jesus spoke about continually. It was the light within that matters, he said. "When your eyes are sound, you have light for your whole body, but when the eyes are bad you are in darkness." He had no time for ceremonial observances—reminders of God—that were merely a cover for a life of darkness within. If you had been able to ask him the question: "What makes you think of God?" he would surely not have answered: "The ritual of handwashing, the pinnacles of the Temple, the preaching of the rabbis," but "Everything"—because his whole inner being was possessed by the Father's love.

None of us is anywhere near that state of inner communion, but this is where we must begin if we want naturally, and at any time, to think of God. In the heart. "Blessed are the pure in heart: for they shall see God." Whether or not a beautiful sunset, an unselfish act, an unexpected joy, or a profound sorrow makes you think of God will depend on whether you have already nourished his communion with him in your heart.

How is such a communion born and fostered? The great majority of us would have to admit that we learned to think of God, to know his inner presence, by what we learned and absorbed in childhood. That is why, after "These commandments are to be kept in your heart," we read: "You shall repeat them to your sons, and speak of them indoors and out of doors, when you lie down and when you rise." No matter how instinctive the thought of God may be for human beings in every age and place, it remains true that the habit of thinking about God, of acknowledging his presence, of being in communion with him, largely depends on our early environment. It is not only in communist countries today that children are being raised without a sense of gratitude and obligation to a heavenly Father. We cannot expect children to think much about God or have any sense of inner communion with him, if nothing in the home, in the attitude of parents, or in early training reflects such an attitude or belief.

We all have an obligation here. If indeed we inherited this habit of thought, no matter how strong or weak it may be, it is our duty to pass it on. I am not talking of brainwashing a child or trying to enforce the same kind of religious experience that was ours. Today's children may not come to this sense of God or the attraction of Jesus just as we did. What matters is not the inculcation of specific beliefs so much as the sense a child will have that the grown-ups around acknowledge a higher power than their own will. It is a spirit of reverence, above all, that can be communicated.

Now we come to something so mundane, so routine, so physical, that Protestants have always had difficulty in understanding it. "Bind them as a sign on the hand and wear them as a phylactery on the forehead; write them up on the doorposts of your houses and your gates." What is all this about? It is a direction to inscribe verses like this one about loving God with heart and soul and strength on strips of paper to bind around the hand, or to put them inside little wooden boxes to be fixed at certain times between the eyes, and to hang them on doorposts. We have moved from the high mystery of divine communion in the heart to practical matters—what you might call little gadgets to remind us of God.

I have traveled with an Orthodox Jewish friend who always wears the skullcap, or yarmulke, wherever he is; and with a Roman Catholic friend who crosses himself before meals. If you asked them what this peculiar habit means, you would be told by the Orthodox Jew that the covering of the head is to remind him of the constant presence of the transcendent God, and by the Catholic that the sign of the cross is a constant reminder of what we owe to Jesus Christ who died for us.

We Protestants have been quick to point out that outward signs are no guarantee of inward reality, that they can be substitutes for the true religion of the heart, that Jesus warned against outward demonstrations of piety, and so on. Yet, are we so sure of our superior acknowledgment of God? Have we such true inward communion that we need no physical reminders of his presence? Does the Bible really condemn all such aids to devotion and not just their abuse? And has not each one of us, in fact, found certain physical objects—a favorite Bible, a picture, a beloved church building, or a special corner of the countryside—to be for us sacraments of the presence of God? And that word sacrament reminds us that the New Testament gospel of the incarnate Son of God is no purely "spiritual" religion, but one of the Word made flesh, or the divine revealed in the human, of the spiritual penetrating the material.

So I would suggest that as we ponder this question: "What makes you think of God?" we should not merely seek to renew the inner communion of the heart, or accept our obligation to pass on what we have received, but that we should also cherish those outward signs that have been for us reminders of the God we so easily forget—and perhaps discover new ways in which some familiar object or action can become our own personal reminders. Let us be honest enough to confess that there is little enough in our daily round to swing our thoughts towards the divine, and devise our own rituals to keep the soul alive. If a glance at a picture or photograph can arouse such thoughts, if the weekly trek to a certain pew does it for you, if stretching your arms as you wake can become a motion of praise to the Lord—then look, and stretch, and trek. On the night in which he was betrayed, Jesus took a towel and washed the disciples' feet. If that had been your towel would it ever have been the same again? And have you no towel at home—in the bathroom or the kitchen—that can be for you a reminder of Jesus?

6

An Expanding Faith in a Contracting World

"He that spared not his own Son, but delivered him up for us all, how shall he not with him also freely give us all things?"

ROMANS 8:32

Perhaps some think a more suitable title for a message today would be "A Contracting Faith in an Expanding World." For the picture they live with is of an advancing, dynamic, secular society, rapidly mastering the secrets of nature, extending its control over every aspect of human behavior, even the boundary mysteries of birth and death, and reaching out to the stars; and within this expanding world diminishing pockets of religion in which some are clinging to the shrinking faith of their fathers. It is the world that is thrusting out towards new horizons while religion is on the retreat. God is a kind of anachronistic indulgence like the childhood teddy bear an adolescent is reluctant to give up.

It would be easy enough to demolish this view of our vanishing religion. If it is based on the declining statistics of church membership in the Western world, it can be countered by the exact opposite figures in Africa, Indonesia, and Korea. If it is based on the successful establishment of officially atheistic societies in about a quarter of the world, one can point to the admitted concern of communist parties at the failure of their propaganda and the persistence of religious belief. If it is based on the theory that modern Western men and women have outgrown any belief in the supernatural, can this be taken seriously at a time when on the one hand thousands of the leaders of our scientific revolution are convinced Christian believers, and on the other hand the whole nation is exploding with every kind of cult from yoga to astrology?

What I really want to question is the notion of the expanding world. This is a more difficult question to get hold of. Of course, there has been an enormous expansion of our knowledge of the universe and a bewildering extension of technology. The horizons of our thinking have receded so fast that now we are prepared to accept almost anything as possible for mankind.

Yet I would maintain that the fundamental fact about the world we know is its contraction. Whether you are talking about entropy, which the dictionary defines as "the degradation of the matter and energy in the universe to a state of inert uniformity," or about the psalmist's reflection on human life: "As for man, his days are as grass; . . . the wind passeth over it, and it is gone; and the place thereof shall know it no more," the world as we know it contracts for every one of us. The biblical reminder still stands that death writes its terminus upon even the most brilliant brain, and upon every generation, including our own. And if we live within the confines of a merely secular world the ultimate vista is the closing curtain: "Out, out, brief candle."

The signs of this contraction are with us today. For the very achievements of which we boast are threatening to make this world a narrower and narrower arena in which to live. Not only does the nuclear energy we have tapped bring all mankind together into the "valley of the shadow of death," but every advance in technology seems to endanger our dignity and freedom. Is the world really expanding and liberated when we are increasingly manipulated by anonymous forces, when enormous powers can pass into violent hands, when our brains can be washed, our life history computerized, our opinions processed, and our conversations bugged? Is Aleksandr Solzhenitsyn not correct to claim that it is the artist who "realizes that there is a supreme force above him and works gladly away as a small apprentice under God's heaven," who can expand his soul in what he calls "this cruel, dynamic, explosive world that stands at the edge of its ten dooms"? And is this not true for us all? The point of hope in a contracting world is precisely where there is an expanding faith.

But is our faith expanding? What kind of God are we clinging to? Somehow we seem to have allowed this all-embracing, all-competent, organizing secular society to push us into a corner, like the space allotted for religious news in the Saturday newspaper. On the whole this is a tolerant age. Everybody can keep his teddy bear if he wants to. It is just not expected to affect our judgment, our behavior, our participation in the daily dance of a secularized society. Have you noticed that hardly anyone, for instance, asks about the religion of a political candidate any more? We call this a triumph of toleration. It may really signify the end of the belief that a person's religion could possibly affect his functioning as a citizen or politician. To ignore a candidate's religion is to indicate that it matters no more than the color of his hair or his taste in ties.

Nowhere in the Bible is our communion with God treated as a special department of life. These books range over the entire spectrum of human existence, and they never suggest that religion is a kind of spare-time interest for those who have a taste for it. In fact, the word "religion" hardly occurs. The faith the Bible proclaims animates all that makes us human—family life, political life, business, housekeeping, physical health, poverty, hunger, the administration of justice, care for the infirm and old, science, the arts, everything. It is the most expansive conception of faith the world has ever known. It is this we have to recapture—a faith that illuminates every activity, every interest, and every corner of the mind.

But, of course, such faith has a center. A Christian, or a church, that forgets this may be tempted to identify a general concern about all these questions with the gospel itself. There is a specific reason, a specific motivation for the Christian's interest and action in every area of life. Perhaps you have seen the radarscopes weathermen show us on TV. I am never quite sure what they are really telling us, but I am fascinated by the little arm that travels around lighting up the landscape. From its center it swings around, and each segment of the territory is illuminated as it passes. Christian faith has a center. But it is not a little point of light to be cherished occasionally when we close our eyes in prayer. It is a dynamic center from which faith covers everything in sight.

And this is where Paul's words strike home with power: "He that spared not his own Son, but delivered him up for us all. . . ." This is the God in whom we believe. The burning center of our faith is this self-giving God—"He that spared not his own Son." What brings us to worship is the summons of a Love that moves the universe and yet was concentrated in one we call Jesus who gave his life for us. This is the gospel, the news, not just that God is love, but that he "so loved the world that he gave his only-begotten Son that whosoever believes in him should not perish but have everlasting life." *Should not perish*—should be released from the iron laws of this contracting world; *have everlasting life*—not just an endless extension of existence but a new quality of life that works from within to transform our whole environment and has the capacity for endless growth.

At the center, then, we yield to this Christ and are touched by the healing power of the Father's love. In our place of worship we listen week by week to the empowering word There the gospel is declared in life-giving symbols—the cleansing water of baptism and the nourishing bread and wine. There we each find our way of responding in faith to the one who says: "As the Father hath loved me, so have I loved you: continue ye in my love."

This is not something that happens in a little spiritual corner and is tucked away under the rubric of religion. What I want to ask now is whether from this center the beam is sweeping out to cover the whole of life as we know it. "He that spared not his own Son, but delivered him up for us all, *how shall he not with him also freely give us all things!*" We are not truly hearing the message of God's love in Christ unless we see it spreading from the cross to embrace everything that meets us every day of the week. Is ours an expanding faith?

He has freely given us all things. Nothing is excluded from the sweep of a living faith. We are not told that he has given us some little area of religion to be cultivated. All things are within the province of the gospel. A look at the activities of many churches today will show a surprising number of things going on—at random you may find swimming, children's games, film programs, task forces on racism, housing, and drugs, employment counseling. A stranger scanning these activities might be tempted to say: "What's all this? Is it a social club with religious overtones?" But I hope he would soon find much more than that. The church is concerned with "all things" because at the burning center of its life is the Christ whose love and service impel us to claim every aspect of life as his Kingdom.

In our contracting world we are given the possibility of an expanding faith. This faith that is rooted in the God "who spared not his own Son, but delivered him up for us all" must claim "all things" as its province. This text challenges us to ask if our faith is really expanding. We all tend to express our faith in one or two particular concerns. Are we being blind to others? I sometimes feel it would be good if every Christian would switch for a year from one particular interest to another. The beam of the radarscope could light up another area, and faith would expand. Do we really believe that there is *no* area of our lives that cannot be so illuminated—our domestic duties, our hobbies, our political opinions, our health, our joy in the arts?

"How shall he not also with him freely give us all things"—what an inheritance! The faith that accepts the gift of God in Christ is meant to expand through every area of our contracting world. God says to all believers: "All things are yours . . . the world, life, death, or things present, or things to come; all are yours; and ye are Christ's; and Christ is God's."

7

The Vote of the Dead

"God is not God of the dead but of the living; for him they are all alive."

LUKE 20:38

"They are all alive"—Abraham, Isaac, Jacob, Moses, Peter, John, Augustine, Luther, Calvin, Knox, our own forefathers. For God they are all alive. Really alive. That is not my guess or pious hope. It is the plain statement of Jesus Christ.

In Luke's day, as in ours, there were those who flatly denied any such possibility. When we die, we die, they said, and that is the end of the story. That was, for instance, the position of the Sadducees. They ruled out any hope of a new life beyond the grave as sentimental nonsense. Against them stood that much maligned body of believing Jews called Pharisees, who affirmed their belief in resurrection. In between there were probably thousands who, like many today, were content to be agnostic. "Who knows?" they said; "perhaps—and perhaps not."

Jesus came down flatly on the side of the Pharisees. What impresses me most about his attitude is that this is the only occasion in which he comes near to arguing the point. Otherwise he just assumes it. Every line of his teaching implies that what we do now has repercussions in a life beyond, and he treats every person he meets as one who has infinite value and an eternal destiny. He speaks more about heaven than any writer in the Bible. Only here, where he is faced with a trick question by the Sadducees does he come close to reasoning out his conviction. And his argument does not simply turn on a little point of grammar—the fact that the Bible says: "I *am* the God of Abraham" and not "I *was.*" It rests on his profound conviction that those who are here and now in touch with the living God will not drop into oblivion when their earthly days are over. "For him they are all alive."

In the great prayer recorded in John 17 we read: "This is life eternal, that they might know thee the only true God, and Jesus Christ, whom thou hast sent." Anyone who has experienced in any way the truth of these words does not need arguments or psychic evidences, and is impervious to the dogmas of materialism. To know God is to know him forever. When I was in Moscow recently our Intourist guide explained why so few Russians go to church. "Most people don't worship," she said, "for, you see, Lenin did not believe in God." It was perhaps false politeness that stopped me from saying: "Well, he does now." Living close to Jesus Christ should give us the same calm and bold assurance about eternal life. Every pastor knows the moment when one is looked straight in the eye and asked for some real hope that death is not the end. I know of no better anchor at such a time than this conviction of Jesus and all who have reflected his gospel in their own lives that the Father we know now is our Father forever. "For him they are all alive."

Yes; but alive where? and alive how? Jesus' answer to the story about the woman who had seven husbands clearly implies that we are incapable here and now of understanding the conditions of life in the eternal dimension. Just as there is a whole area of our human life that is hidden from the animal world—even your favorite dog cannot share your appreciation of a beautiful sunset or a masterpiece of art, or your moral dilemmas, your ambitions, your politics, or your religion—so there must be strict limits to what we can now know about the where and the how of life beyond the grave. But I think we are not left in total ignorance about the activities of the dead. Nothing in the words of Jesus and his apostles suggests that they live on in some remote sphere where they can exert no influence whatever on the world we know. For them the "happy land" is not "far, far away." They are alive—and they are near.

I want now to explore the impact of the dead on our lives today. It seems to me that there are many exciting and neglected aspects of the truth we express when we say: "I believe in the communion of saints." The title "The Vote of the Dead" is intended to indicate a belief that the dead have a voice in our affairs right now. It would be good for this self-contained generation, so obsessed with the immediate and so apt to be contemptuous of that which is vanished from sight, to listen again to this voice from beyond.

We can begin at a point where everyone must agree, whatever his views about eternity. The vote of the dead operates biologically. None of us can escape the impact of heredity. The dance of the genes in our system is affecting our decisions all the time. Without in any way accepting the theory that everything is predetermined by this hereditary factor, we cannot escape this secret ballot of our ancestors. As we get older we continually find ourselves reflecting the habits and opinions of our parents and grandparents. A man in his fifties may be startled to find that what he is saying to his son is just what used to infuriate him when he heard it from his father. This vote of the dead is with us whether we like it or not, and the Bible was outspoken about it long before the days of biological science. The phrase from the Ten Commandments that sounds so offensive in religious ears: "for I the Lord thy God am a jealous God, visiting the iniquity of the fathers upon the children unto the third and fourth generation of them that hate me" is just a vivid way of expressing the brute fact of the biological impact of the dead—for good or evil.

Everyone also recognizes that the dead have a vote through the writings, the works of art, the institutions they have bequeathed us. We are being influenced every day of our lives by this heritage, and it is an impoverished generation that neglects it. In all the jargon about the "meaningful" and the "relevant" there hides a thin and arrogant assumption that this voice of the dead has nothing to say to this unique generation. Even the churches, which should be more sensitive to this inheritance than any other community, have been infected and distracted by the passion for the Now.

As we move from the biological to the truly human, something new comes to light in this vote of the dead. We begin to glimpse the meaning of that vote, which way it is being cast. For it is evident that out of the vast creative efforts of the past generations only a fraction has remained to influence us now. And that fraction represents, almost without exception, the highest human values—the true, the beautiful, and the good. Bluntly speaking, the rubbish has fallen away into the cosmic garbage dump, while that which enlightens and inspires has endured. There was plenty of pornography being written in ancient Greece, but it is Plato who is read today. There was a lot of trashy music being written in eighteenth-century Germany, but it is Mozart we are listening to. There were bucketfuls of bad theology being written in fourth-century Christendom, but the Nicene Creed still stands. There were dozens of wild-eyed fanatics around at the time of the Reformation, but Luther and Calvin are still casting their vote in the church today.

Have you ever wondered about the way we tend to think chiefly about the virtues of the dead we have known and not of their vices? Is it simply sentiment and good taste that lie behind the saying *De mortuis nil nisi bonum* ("Speak nothing but good of the dead")? May it not be that there is a purifying spirit that breathes through from the eternal world assuring us that it is the good, the true, and the beautiful that endure? Are we not told that faith, hope and love *abide*—go on forever—and the "greatest of these is love?" Without pretending to believe that every man or woman by the mere fact of dying is immediately transformed into a perfect saint, we can surely sense that their vote from the eternal world is now entirely on the side of love and life and joy and peace.

And that leads to the thrilling possibilities opened up by the Christian doctrine of the communion of the saints and the tremendous implications of the words: "For him they are all alive." We have now moved far beyond the biological or the historical. The dead, according to the gospel, are not influencing us simply because their blood flows in our veins and their noblest works are still with us. They are actually alive. With this assertion the Christian breaks with every philosophy or religion that merely honors their memory or extols their works. "Because he lives, we shall live also." That has been the Christian conviction ever since the news broke that Jesus had risen from the dead. And the accent is on *live.* Just as it was no pale ghost that came back from the dead, just as it is no vague influence that Jesus exerts on those who believe in him but a dynamic presence, so the dead are fully alive, more alive than they ever were on earth. That is the stupendous assertion of the New Testament.

The vote of the dead, then, is a living voice for all who have ears to hear. The early Christians had this sense of the nearness of the eternal world, and they expressed it in the rich imagery and flaming words of their faith: "You stand before Mount Zion and the city of the living God, heavenly Jerusalem, before myriads of angels, the full concourse and assembly of the first-born citizens of heaven." "You *stand*"—not "You will stand." At every service of worship they were conscious that they were not alone but surrounded by the company of heaven. In their daily life and decisions they would realize the indwelling vote of the dead and were uplifted by their prayers.

"They are all alive." This is where I want to raise a question. When we struggle to share in this Christian hope, when we pause to realize in worship or in private prayer the presence of those whom we have loved on earth, how do we think of them? I have already remarked that we tend to think positively not negatively, but do we think of them exclusively *as they were?* Have we frozen them, as it were, in the postures and convictions we knew at their best? Do we assume that their vote today would be exactly as we could have foretold it long ago? If so we have not really heard the words: "They are all alive." For life means growth, development. If Martin Luther at death was frozen into his thoughts and convictions of 1546, in what way could he be called alive today?

This is what I find heretical about the hyperorthodox Protestants of today. At every proposed change they fulminate about betraying the heritage of Calvin or Knox. They thereby indicate that they do not really believe in the kind of eternal life promised in the gospel. For they assume that Calvin and Knox are somewhere in heaven, clothed in their ancient garb, clutching their ancient volumes, and biting their nails over the changes in the church today. My picture is completely different, for I believe that the Reformers are alive—and that, therefore, they are at least as up-to-date as we. Luther, Calvin, and Knox are right now on the side of everything that makes the grace of our Lord Jesus Christ, the love of God, and the communion of the Holy Spirit, real and active in the lives of the ordinary man or woman today. They are reminding us of the eternal and unchanging gospel, but they are not casting their votes for the eternal status quo.

May I gently suggest that all of us need to update our image of our own beloved dead? If we have ever found ourselves thinking, or even saying: "*Now* she understands"; "*Now* he'll know it all," then we are on the right track. For we are groping after the conviction that the dead are truly alive, and moving with us into the future but with much clearer eyes. If we think of them in the biblical image as "a cloud of witnesses," they are not just spectators from a distance of one, ten, fifty, or four hundred years; they are contemporaries cheering us on. We sing their songs, and they are singing ours. And in our efforts to steer the right course, to win through to the fulfilment God has planned for us, their vote is being cast all the time on the side of love, of courage, of hope, of justice, of integrity and faith. Can we hear it again? "For God they are all *alive*."

8

Can We All Have Faith?

"Don't be afraid; only believe."

MARK 5:36

That is the basic word of Jesus for every human being in every age. That is how he lived—with faith and without fear—and that is the program for all of us who claim in any way to be his followers today.

"Don't be afraid, only believe." He is talking about something that is as real for us as it was for the anxious father of the little girl in the story. We know a lot more about the universe and the way it works than he did, but that knowledge has not reduced our fears. As we grow up we discard some of the fears of childhood only to discover that greater understanding and wider responsibilities can enlarge the area of our fears. A child may be afraid of a shadow cast on the wall by a flickering light but knows nothing of the shadows cast on the adult mind by the real dangers that threaten our welfare or our very existence, or the ultimate fear that hovers over our sophisticated society—that life makes no sense, has no direction or meaning, and that death is oblivion. Jesus is not talking about the peculiar beliefs of religious people. He is not even talking about only this specific example of faith—the belief that he could cure the little girl. His words go to the center of your life and mine. Basically, when we think ahead or when we are hit by one of life's cruelest blows, do we have faith—or are we afraid?

If Jesus had been speaking about faith as the capacity to accept a lot of religious ideas that many people find incredible, he would have said something different—"Don't be a skeptic, only believe," or "Don't ever have any doubts, only believe." That is the contrast many people have in mind when they think of the difference between those who go to church on Sunday morning and the many others who have nothing to do with the church. It is a matter of temperament, they say, or of the way we were raised. Some find it easy to accept religious beliefs like those expressed in the Apostles' Creed; others find it impossible. So we hear remarks like: "He's very religious," or "She's not a church kind of person," or "I'm afraid I'm not the believing type."

If you read the Gospels without any of this kind of prejudice, you will find that Jesus never divided human beings into the religious and the nonreligious. If there is such a distinction to be found in these pages we cannot help noticing that he seemed more drawn to the nonreligious. For he found many religious people so sealed off by the minutiae and mechanics of their faith that they could not hear what he was saying about our basic needs and how they can be met. And he found that many skeptics, nonconformists and religious rebels knew what he was talking about when he said that he had come "to seek and to save that which was lost." It was not temperament or training that inclined a man or woman to accept or to reject his gospel. It was solely their willingness to confess their lostness—the fears, the emptiness, the aimlessness of life without meaning—and to accept his assurance of the reality, the nearness and the eternal love of a Father-God that drew them to him. And such attraction could be sparked in anyone at all—from a rabbi to a Roman centurion, from a dutiful housewife like Martha to the bantering lady at the well of Samaria who was a quintuple divorcee.

"*Only* believe." That word "only" gets to us. He makes it sound so simple. We feel like saying: "But believing for me is the hardest thing in the world. I'm not naturally disposed to believe in anything except what I see or what can be proved. Belief in a real God, belief in a mysterious

81

healing power, belief in a life beyond the grave is terribly difficult. What do you mean '*only* believe?' " And we think, perhaps enviously, of people we know who seem to find it easy.

But Jesus knew human nature better than we do. He knew that the capacity for belief, for faith, is the very quality that makes us human. Belief has no meaning in the vegetable and very little in the animal world. A tree in the park does not *believe* that the leaves it sheds in the fall will be replaced in the spring. It just happens. A cow grazes, and chews, and produces milk without any inspiring ambition that some day she will jump over the moon. A dog, through long association with the human race, will learn the meaning of trust, but could hardly be said to be inspired and directed by some vision of the unseen and eternal. But to be human is to be a believer. In every generation someone will come along to prove that we are, after all, just vegetable or animal, that we are simply reacting to a more complicated series of controls. Yet even those who would rule out all human faith and vision as some kind of automatic reflex are usually inconsistent enough to appeal to us to *believe* their theory. We are believers by nature. The essence of our humanity is to choose to devote ourselves to one way of life rather than another.

Julian Huxley, who is not a Christian believer, or even a theist, expressed it this way:

Anyone who has experienced the illumination of new knowledge, or the ecstasy of poetry or music, or the deliberate subordination of self for something greater, or the self-abandonment of falling in love, or complete physical well-being, or the intense satisfaction of a difficult task achieved, or has had any mystical experience, knows that they are in some way valuable for their own sakes, beyond ordinary everyday satisfactions, such as being just moderately fit, earning one's own living, or filling one's belly.

In this sense we are all believers, and the greatest leaders of the human race have been the greatest believers in some ideal or cause beyond the sight of their eyes or the logic of their minds. But what was the content of the specific belief that Jesus was speaking about? I believe I can best express it by using a phrase from Paul—"the power of God for salvation." He is asking us to believe in the reality of a God of love who is in ultimate control of everything, and whose healing and rescuing power is available to all who trust him. A true Christian is marked off from others by a belief in this "power of God" as it meets us in Jesus. That is why Paul underlined the necessity for faith. "I am not ashamed," he said, "of the gospel: it is the power of God for salvation *to every one who has faith.*" The power is there—just as the space around is full of invisible impulses that affect us not at all until we switch on a radio and turn them into music. Faith is our tuning in to the unseen power of God. Faith is our personal reception of a presence that is always there.

So when Jesus says "only believe," he is not just offering a theory or proposition for us to accept. He is talking about a God who wants our personal trust and love. Another name for this "power of God for salvation" is the little word "grace." Grace is God coming alongside to help. Grace is what we experience when we look into the face of Jesus and know that God is reflected there, a God who loves us in spite of our sins, and a God who can transform us into the likeness of his Son, and who can see us through anything that can happen in life and death. "By grace," says the Bible, "are you saved through faith." Grace is like the hand of God thrust out towards us through the darkness: faith is our hand that lets itself be held.

So when I hear the word "faith," I think not chiefly of the great resounding creeds of the church in which our beliefs are enshrined nor of struggling to accept a philosophy that hooks on to nothing in my mind or my experience. I think of the intimate kind of trust that a child has in his mother or an adult in a beloved friend—the kind of person we turn to in a crisis. That is why at the center of this vast network called the Christian church there is a Person. It is Jesus, who knows what this life is like and what can be made of it, who knows every danger that can threaten, every pang we can suffer, who has been through death to the other side. It is Jesus who says: "Don't be afraid: only have faith." I would rather trust him than anyone else.

There is no one way in which to express that trust. And so there is, I believe, no single human being who is excluded by temperament of training from faith in him. In this story from which the text is taken two very different people respond to him. Jairus I see as the intellectual, a leader of the synagogue, trained in the Hebrew Scriptures, the last person, in many ways, to be attracted to the unconventional and disturbing young preacher from Nazareth. Yet at a point of deep human need, with his daughter mortally ill, he responds, not as an intellectual or a member of the establishment, but as a desperately distressed father. "My little daughter is at death's door. I beg you to come and lay your hands on her to cure her and save her life." Nothing else mattered—his temperament, his training, his prejudices, his prestige. He was just a human being in need, letting his heart speak as Jesus drew from him a deep and unexpected trust.

The woman in the crowd I see as a totally different personality—ignorant, perhaps slightly hysterical, shriveled in body and soul by years of hemorrhages. For her there is no confrontation with Jesus and no intellectual prejudices to be overcome. She acts impulsively. She does not believe that she is important enough to talk to

Jesus. She knows nothing save her instinct that in him is this "power of God." So her act of trust found no expression in words. It was nothing more than a gesture. "She came up from behind the crowd and touched his cloak." That was all. And it was enough. Enough to make Jesus stop, "aware that power had gone out of him." Enough to make him say, "My daughter, your faith has cured you."

This is why I believe that faith is for all, that there is no one who is sealed off from the approach of Jesus. I am convinced that there is no individual, no generation, no segment of society, for whom a response to Christ is for any reason impossible. He can walk into any heart, at any time, and say, "Don't be afraid; only believe."

We are different enough in our moods, and in our needs. But around the Lord's Table we support one another in an act of trust. Whether we are communing with one who has become to us as real and near as any human friend or are almost blindly reaching out to touch his cloak, that is the moment to receive him, as we touch, and eat and drink. He holds out the bread and the wine saying: "Don't be afraid; only believe."

9

When Love Gets Tired

"If your brother wrongs you, rebuke him; and if he repents, forgive him. Even if he wrongs you seven times in a day and comes back to you seven times saying, 'I am sorry,' you are to forgive him."

"The apostles said to the Lord, 'Increase our faith.' "

LUKE 17:4, 5 NEB

There is an awkward moment in every preacher's experience. He has just delivered a sermon on Christian love, spelling out its obligations, stressing its practicality and its application to every human being no matter how depraved or unlovable. Those who greet him at the close of the service murmur words like "beautiful" and "inspirational." The coffee hour is all sweetness and light. But when he finally puts on his coat and makes his way out of the church he spots a furtive character lurking in the doorway, the sight of whom immediately extinguishes the inward glow. For he knows almost exactly what this stranger is going to tell him. He is stranded in New York with a sick wife waiting for him in Albany, Chicago, or San Francisco (according to his estimate of the pastor's resources). And, of course, on a Sunday all the agencies of relief are closed.

What does our preacher do? The tempting answer is to do a quick reverse and exit by another door. Then, unless his skin is illegitimately thick, his conscience pricks him all the way home as phrases from his sermon rise up to torment him and charge him with hypocrisy. And the same thing may happen if he stops and listens to the story and then coldly informs the suppliant that there is nothing doing. But if, on the other hand, he listens sympathetically and then hands over money with a smile and a blessing, can he be sure that he has done the right thing and really put his sermon into practice? Conscience again says: "Ah! Easy way out; and you have just contributed to the downfall of a panhandler who will proceed to milk another pastor even less able to afford it. Is that Christian love?"

I raise the question simply to illustrate the fact that it is not only the man in the pew who finds difficulty in translating fine words into appropriate action. Every one of us knows of the tension that exists between the rhetoric and the reality of Christian love. There is no more agonizing problem for the church today than this widespread impression that what we hear and pray and sing in church has little to do with the decisions we have to make in business, in politics, in chance encounters, or even in the home. The rhetoric of the pulpit seems to belong to a happy land far away, where we all agree that love is wonderful and where it sounds as if we were called to make a simple choice between what is clearly the right action and what is certainly the wrong. But the reality is that the way of love is often much more worrisome than wonderful, and the choice seldom seems as easy as it sounds in church.

This contrast hit me forcibly when as a young preacher I found myself a chaplain in a POW camp. In circumstances of close confinement and enforced proximity there is little chance for mere rhetoric to be greeted with pious enthusiasm. Every statement was under scrutiny by men sharing the same privations and exposed to the same temptations as the preacher. There is nothing like intimate contact day by day and night by night for throttling down the oratory! I am not saying that we found the Christian gospel unworkable and ineffective. On the contrary, the New Testament came to life on occasion much as Ernest Gordon has described in his moving book

Through the Valley of the Kwai. But we learned something of the tough decisions that love requires. Suppose, for instance, you are in a little cell with three others and normally eat at a little table opposite one of them. The authorities decide not to issue daily bread but to give each prisoner a loaf to last the week. You measure off a seventh and put the remainder carefully away each day. The man opposite you does what you all long to do: he bolts the entire loaf on the first day. After two or three days, as you see him watching you consume your allotted portion, do you give him some?—thus making sure he will do the same thing next time around? Or, let us say, you are fortunate enough one day to receive a private parcel that contains one slab of chocolate. Divided among two hundred it would mean nothing. Divided among four it would be a treat for all. Or do you go into a quiet corner and consume the whole thing? Perhaps that one is easier; in any case, you can see how on occasion a sermon would come home to roost.

The first thing I have to say about this tension between our Christian ideals and practice is this: if you are troubled by the contrast between the rhetoric and the reality, if you are often puzzled about the really loving course of action, *thank God!* For the most devastating disease that can infect a church or a Christian soul is a paralysis of conscience, an inability to see where we fall short, or a comfortable conviction that there is no real agony of decision. The real Christian is not the one who is satisfied with his level of performance and tells you glibly that he lives by the Sermon on the Mount (oddly enough, it is usually the nonchurchgoer who makes that remark!), but the one who knows what it really means to confess our failures in love and to pray God in his mercy to forgive what we have been, amend what we are, and direct what we shall be.

This means that we know that the way of love is no soft and sentimental road, and that it offers no easy answers. But it also means that we believe in an inexhaustible grace that forgives our failures and constantly empowers us to do better. That is the liberating hope of the gospel, which reaches us just when we need it; for our love, we know, is very exhaustible. That is why I am concentrating now on just one aspect of the life of love—our tendency to get tired, to compromise, to settle for something less than the demands of Jesus.

His commandment of love has nothing to do with the kind of blinkered benevolence that sees no evil and tries to smother everyone in a genial embrace. It is a commandment precisely because it can be obeyed by an act of the will—and no act of the will can enable me to like everybody that crosses my path or to feel emotionally drawn to them. The love he teaches and exemplifies is a strong and resolute desire for the welfare of others, a refusal to indulge in hatred or revenge, a willingness to forgive again and again, a concern—

even for our opponents—that means we desire nothing but good for them.

William Barclay has summed up Jesus' message like this:

It would be impossible to demand that we love our enemies as we love those who are dearer to us than love itself. But it is possible to say to us: "You must try to be like God. You must try never to wish anything but good for others. You must try to look at every man with the eyes of God, with the eyes of goodwill."

This is what has dazzled and astonished the world in the life of Jesus himself. The Gospels do not show us a mild and mushy idealist talking of a fantasy world in which everyone is lovable. He is an immensely strong character who, as the record says, "knew what was in man" and is not afraid to call a spade a spade—as when he referred to Herod Antipas as "that fox." But with all his insight into the evil around him and what it might eventually do to him, he unswervingly sought the best for every man, woman, and child who crossed his path—without any regard for their worthiness in the eyes of men. His was a love that never tired, even when the establishment unleashed its fury against him, even when his own friends disappointed him by their frailty and folly and deserted him in his hour of need. From the agony of the cross he looked down at the taunting priests, the callous soldiers, and the blood-thirsty crowd and cried: "Father, forgive them; for they know not what they do." And, as for the disciples, who were cowering in their hiding places, we are told that "having loved his own which were in the world, he loved them unto the end."

It is this kind of love that he never ceased to commend to his disciples with a wealth of startling illustrations and epigrams. Since he knew very well how easily we lose heart when we try to practice this kind of caring and concern, he shocked his disciples with this remark one day: "If your brother wrongs you, rebuke him; and, if he repents, forgive him. Even if he wrongs you seven times in a day and comes back to you seven times, saying, 'I am sorry,' you are to forgive him."

He is obviously not talking about someone whom it is easy to love and to forgive. I had a letter recently in which a friend who has done a lot of social work talked of the difference between the "attractive" sinner, or person with a problem, and the "chronic" who tries your patience. "How your heart sinks," she wrote, "when a certain person asks for an appointment or phones." Jesus is surely here talking about the chronic. How long are we supposed to go on accepting, forgiving, trying to help? And the answer, in the form of the mystic number seven, is "for ever."

Notice that in this case, where real wrong has been done to you, Jesus does not gloss over the fault. He uses the words "rebuke" and "repent." Love involves an element of toughness in dealing with the chronic—how else would love seek the best for him? What is ruled out is not only anger and rejection, but simply giving up. Like Jesus, having loved, we are to love unto the end.

This applies, of course, not just to people who cross our path as what we call "problem cases," but to the most intimate relationships in the home or at work. It is the difficult person whom we have to go on loving in this way. "Love is patient," says Paul in his exquisite interpretation of the love of Christ; "love is kind and envies no one. Love is never boastful nor conceited, nor rude; never selfish, not quick to take offense. Love keeps no score of wrongs; does not gloat over other men's sins. . . ."

If we really hear that, we shall be delivered from a wrong construction of this word of Jesus about continuing to forgive. For it is possible to accept this commandment in a smug and self-satisfied way, assuming that all the wrong is on the other side. I sometimes get letters in which a spouse or a parent writes about his constant forbearance toward and forgiveness of an erring mate or child. Behind the lines is an assumption that the writer's own behavior is immaculate. As in such counseling problems I want equal time for the other party! "Love keeps no score of wrongs."

This is a tough assignment. The disciples were overwhelmed. And their response is striking. "Lord," they said, "increase our faith." That seems a little odd at first sight. One would expect "increase our love." But there it is: "Increase our *faith.*" It is worth pondering that this expression does not come after Jesus had been speaking about matters of doctrine and belief. If he had been expounding, for example, the dogma of the Trinity or the mystery of his Person, we should have found it natural for them to ask for an increase of faith. But it was when they were faced with the demands of an absolute and untiring love that they made this request.

At least they had begun to see what Jesus meant by faith, a discovery that many have still to make. For he had made it clear that faith is trust in a God of total and untiring love. The more we know and rely on this God, who is willing to accept us as we are, who does not demand that we reach a certain level of goodness in order to be forgiven, who sheds his love as indiscriminately as the rain that falls on the just and the unjust, and who works in everything for good to them that love him, the more we shall be empowered to love and keep on loving.

This is why we can never separate, as some try to do, the ethics and the devotion of the Christian way. The demands of this untiring love are impossible without the sustaining grace of the God from whom it flows. From the beginning Christians were able to demonstrate this new kind of love to an astonished world because they were in constant touch with the loving God, looking to his Son for inspiration, and knowing the indwelling power of his Spirit. That is still the program for us as we return to the hard task of loving the unlovable, caring for the unattractive, and not giving up on the difficult and demanding. We need most of all an increase in our faith in the God who treats you and me just like that. And there is no better way to increase that faith than to center our lives in prayer, worship, and devotion on Jesus Christ. "Think of him," said the apostle, "who submitted to such opposition from sinners: that will help you not to lose heart and grow faint."

10

"Nothing Left Remarkable Beneath the Visiting Moon?"

"Open thou mine eyes, that I may behold wondrous things out of thy law."

PSALM 119:18

Some will recognize the words of the title. They are spoken by Shakespeare's Cleopatra in the climactic scene when her lover Antony dies in her arms. I can never read them without that shiver in the spine which only the greatest poetry evokes.

The crown o' the earth doth melt. My Lord!
O, withered is the garland of the war,
The soldier's pole is fallen; young boys and girls
Are level now with men; the odds is gone,

And there is nothing left remarkable
Beneath the visiting moon.

Nothing left remarkable—three words in which is enclosed the devastation caused by the loss of a great love. We are not simply responding to a moment of high and distant tragedy from the annals of romantic love. Shakespeare, as usual, touches a universal experience of the human heart. A great bereavement will do this to us all. The death of the beloved not only creates a terrible vacuum in the soul: it seems to drain the meaning and color out of life. It stifles for a while our sense of wonder and of gratitude. We seem unable to respond to the tingle of life around us. Everything in nature and humanity that normally sparkles with interest and excitement, everything that arouses our passions of joy, curiosity, appreciation, or indignation sinks into a twilight gray.

Mercifully, we all know that time is a healer. And Christians know that there is a Lord who has visited that twilight world and has returned alive forevermore. We believe that "because he lives we shall live also"—not only in a heaven beyond but also right here where we find a resurrection of light, color, meaning, and joyful response to the fascinating mystery of the world around us. It is when we are in touch with the eternal, however fragile our faith may be, that this temporal world becomes truly "remarkable" and lights up with meaning and with wonder.

Now let me shift this acute experience of the world going dead to the general malaise of our time. There would be many to tell me that it does not take a great bereavement to induce in them a feeling of dullness and loss of interest in things and people around them. It happens to all of us, from time to time, and the loss of freshness and wonder is typical of our age. This has been a century of brilliant achievement and amazing discoveries, yet as we approach its last quarter the mood is not so much of *Brave New World* as of *The Waste Land.* The triumphs of technology have been so rapid and spectacular that they have ceased to arouse even that thrill which some of us knew when we tickled the cat's whisker on a crystal set and heard our first radio. The first journey to the moon stirred our imaginations and moved some to the depths, but even then I seemed to hear from the younger generation a kind of tired "So what?" Successive landings by brave men, backed by a miracle of technology, found millions giving it a passing glance. Have we reached a saturation-point when no technical achievement will any more evoke a sense of wonder or admiration? Have the French master-cynics given us the last words on the subject—*blasé* and *déjà vu?* Is there nothing left remarkable under—shall we say now—the *visited* moon?

It is clearer than ever that the multiplicity of machines to distract and amuse is providing no answer to boredom, and the prospect of vaster stretches of leisure time looms like a threat. This is why increasing numbers are trying to break through to a dimension of increased awareness, heightened consciousness, and inward illumination either by means of hallucinogenic drugs or some mystic cult. They are tired of a planned society and a scientific culture where everything becomes predictable and nothing is remarkable, and, to the surprise of rationalistic humanists, are asserting again the hunger for miracle and mystery. Clergy and psychiatrists alike agree that this is the new search for God. A psychoanalyst told me flatly that the LSD trip was a question chiefly for the church—not just therapeutically but theologically.

What *is* the role of religion in this search for a richer inward life, for mystery and wonder? It is tempting for the preacher to try to deal with the question of boredom by offering what amounts to psychological advice flavored by a little piety. It is also tempting to make facile statements that the churches offer an experience of the divine that is more genuine and lasting than the "instant God" of the hallucinogenic drugs. But we have to acknowledge that this has not been an area in which the churches have demonstrated great vitality in this generation. In some ways we have been more active than previous generations of churchmen—the church in America has been a more influential body than in any other period since the Founding Fathers. But in this central matter of providing a soul-expanding, mind-blowing, miracle-working experience of God, we have failed.

We have even contributed to the impression that there is "nothing left remarkable beneath the visiting moon." For we have attempted to deal with the question of dullness and boredom by superficial means. We offer helpful formulas for dealing with depression. We try to keep everyone busy. ("My pastor," a man said to me recently, "seems to think that I have a desperate need to be more involved—and I haven't.") Then, at the very point where the real answers are to be found we backtracked. In the name of the mythical "modern mind" we went through fifty years of rationalizing the theology and worship of the church. There was a determined effort in most of the major denominations to divest our proclaimed beliefs of anything that might not be acceptable to this "modern mind," which was presumed to be oriented towards the scientifically provable. Anything that smelled of miracle was silently expunged. In many quarters "supernatural" became a dirty word. Public worship was purged of mystery—both that which is expressed in charismatic freedom and that which is shrouded in the ancient rituals of the church. A way of worship developed in which there is nothing left remarkable—only a sensible, comfortable environment in which to be reasonably religious.

Now the pendulum is swinging again, and we

are trying to catch up with the religious excitement that has broken out in unexpected places. "Excitement" is an in-word today. Anyone who wants to commend a program or an idea to others describes it as "exciting." When in the course of a discussion on worship I hear it said: "We must make our worship more exciting," something in me responds. Worship should be an exciting moment in our week. It should be experience that enlarges the soul, an activity that captivates our whole being. It should be a time when the roof comes off, and we see the seraphim, and hear the "Holy, holy, holy" at the throne of God.

But this is just the point. The true excitement of worship, the real answer to a world in which there is nothing left remarkable, lies in this sense of the overwhelming presence of God. And this is not something we can stage-manage by adopting some of the trappings of other traditions or popular cults, or by jazzing up the ritual with a weekly sensational event. There is nothing sacrosanct about the forms of worship to which we are accustomed, and I am sure these forms will change, perhaps in ways beyond our imagining, in the years ahead. But all true change will be response to the living Spirit of God, and to a great extent it will be a recovery of the glory that already exists in the everlasting gospel and the riches of our heritage since Pentecost. After all, it is not we but God who makes worship exciting, and it is a new vision of the eternal God—a way of communion with him that is real and absorbing for this generation—for which we must pray.

"And there is nothing left remarkable beneath the visiting moon" are Cleopatra's words as her great lover dies. Since the beginning of history mankind has had a love affair with God. There have been moments of ecstasy and fulfilment, and moments of rejection and despair. There has been much hatred mingled with this love. There has been cruel separation and agonizing reconciliation. The story is not by any means one of a steady decline from a primitive paradise of perfect union, through quarrel and bitterness, to an ultimate rejection in which mankind decides that his God is dead. As with mankind, so with each one of us, there is constant change in our relationship with the Father-God. It is not, either for the human race or for you and me, simply a question of what Wordsworth expressed when he said:

Heaven lies about us in our infancy!
Shades of the prison-house begin to close
Upon the growing boy. . . .

Some adults are much nearer to God now than in adolescence. Others may be looking back to a time when God was much more real than he is today. Still others may be conscious right now that a window is opening into a new relationship of trust and joy.

What we can say is that our boredom, our sense of *déjà vu*, our lack of the remarkable, the wonderful, is closely linked with this great love affair, our union with our God. This is by no means the first period in human history when the word goes out that God is dead, but whenever it happens it follows with the devastating logic of the soul that "there is nothing left remarkable beneath the visiting moon." For loving the invisible God lights up the visible world, to be grasped by the eternal is to find the temporal come alive, to have the heavenly vision makes this earth exciting.

If I were hunting for images to illuminate our thoughts of God, it is to the sun I would turn and not to the moon. What happens when a full moon shines out upon us as we walk through a field at night? We think, "How beautiful the moon is," and we know why it was worshiped as the goddess of the sky. There is a kind of moon-worshiping in the devotion that thinks of God as hovering in the heavens for our adoration and desperately tries to form an image of his being. But what happens when the sun is blazing on a fair spring day? If you saw someone standing in the park staring at the sun saying, "How beautiful, how lovely it is," you would be apt to look for the police. This is the discovery we may have to make about this God who loves us. He is to be seen, not directly by a frantic search for the mystic vision, but as we watch the world come to life under his loving and creative touch.

So you might say that the Father-God woos us through the world and the people he has made.

And it is only as we are open and responsive to his wooing that we find both the certainty of his presence and the new awareness of the wonder and excitement of his world. The Bible expresses the longing both of the soul for God—"As the hart panteth after the water brooks, so panteth my soul after thee, O God"—and of God the Father for his prodigal family—"O Lord, thou hast searched me, and known me . . . whither shall I go from thy spirit? or whither shall I flee from thy presence?" But the Bible has little to do with the kind of mysticism that seeks a lone religious ecstasy in total isolation from this world and our neighbors. That is why the biblical vision always contains the word. You can just enjoy a vision. You must respond to a word. Thus when the temple flamed with glory for the young Isaiah the voice pierced through: "Whom shall I send; and who will go for me?" And the vision of John on the island of Patmos, with all its rich symbols of sight and sound, was of the Jesus who had a task for him to do.

"Open thou mine eyes." That is our prayer. It is part of the process of rebirth that the eyes which have been blinded by the traffic of the years may open again with the eagerness and innocence of childhood. "Open thou mine eyes that I may behold wondrous things." This is what we want—to recover the sense of wonder, the deep mysteries in a world where there is not much left that is remarkable. But how does the prayer end? "Out of thy law." A letdown? The old moral bit that religious people cannot shake off? Not at all. The law is the word, the demand of the Lover. It is the prism through which we see the wonders, the test of our readiness to obey. It is the reminder that it is the pure in heart who see their God. It is the warning against a mysticism that numbs our response to human need. But when as Christians we pray this prayer it is not simply the law, the demand of the lover, to which we are responding. For the law becomes grace, and the word becomes flesh in Jesus Christ our Lord. It is he who opens our eyes to behold the wondrous things, and as we strip down to a basic, infant trust, we hear him saying: "I thank thee, O Father, Lord of heaven and earth, that thou hast hid these things from the wise and prudent, and hast revealed them unto babes."

11

Our Search for Believability

"I know whom I have believed . . . "
II TIMOTHY 1:12

If this is Paul, baring his soul, it is not exactly what you would expect him to say. From the great dogmatician of the infant church, from a man who argued his way through countless sermons and letters, from a man who constantly laid his convictions on the line, the natural declaration would be: "I know *what* I have believed." In that shift from "what" to "whom" lies the secret of the gospel that is still hidden from many who find Christianity as a block of dogma as cold and inscrutable as the Sphinx.

Have you noticed that a similar shift is going on in popular speech today? The word "believable" was until recently almost always used about reports, opinions, or convictions. "I find your story quite unbelievable." "That's a believable doctrine." "Mark's account of Jesus seems to me more believable than John's"—that is how the word occurred in ordinary talk. Now it is being applied to persons and their "believability." Suddenly the word is being applied to people in the public eye, and we even find ourselves asking the curious question: "Am I believable?"

Elections are often decided by one simple question: which of the candidates is the most believable? It is, of course, a variant of the old political device of projecting the image of *the man you can trust*. I remember as a boy in Scotland seeing innumerable posters of a rugged, pipe-smoking Stanley Baldwin on every other corner with that slogan attached. But somehow "believability" is being used today with more of a sting. A sophisticated electorate is not looking for a father-figure but for some assurance that, within the limits of politics as "the art of the possible," promise and performance will be more nearly related. The situation is, however, complicated by the fact that as soon as it is recognized that "believability" will win the election, every artifice and subterfuge will be used to project that image on our television screens. There is nothing more unbelievable than synthetic believability.

That raises the question of the crisis of confidence that seems to have come upon us. It is not a matter of politicians and their assurances, but of the whole fabric of our life today. To a much greater extent than we realize, our common life depends on the number of believable people around. A decent society can only tolerate a certain level of skepticism and distrust. An economic system like ours would collapse if we ever reached a point where no one's word could be trusted and no financial statement was believable. We are in danger when more and more citizens find police protection unbelievable and get themselves a gun. Something has gone wrong when the solemn vows of Christian marriage—"in plenty and in want, in joy and in sorrow, in sickness and in health, as long as you both shall live"—become unbelievable because the fundamental trust between bride and groom is no longer there. A rise in the tide of cynicism, as represented in so many movies, plays, and novels, could lead to a submerging of the network of belief and confidence that sustains our common life. If we are to survive as a tolerable society with hopes for the future, we need a renewal of trust, and that means more trustworthy people. That is what I call our search for the believable.

The Bible, as usual, has something to say to us in this crisis of confidence. The entire book could be described as the record of a search by the believable God for believable people. What I mean by that is that the thrust of the Bible from beginning to end is towards the re-creation of a people of God who will live in a spirit of common trust and love because they are sustained by an utterly reliable, believable, and dependable Lord. The dominant word in the Old Testament is one that means "steadfast love," and the constant call is for an utter reliance on that love, and a consequent reflection of it in the practical affairs of the community. That is the call; but the Bible is ruthless in exposing the failure of men and women to respond. The biting words of the prophets about what they term the tendency to go "a-whoring after other gods" are not just the rhetoric of narrow-minded and disappointed preachers. They derive from the insight that without a single-minded trust in one pure, good, and trustworthy God, there is not likely to be much trust and believability in public and private life.

If we think that we are living in the worst of times, we might listen again to the prophet Micah's description of the state into which his people had sunk. "Loyal men have vanished from the earth, there is not one upright man. All lie in wait to do murder; . . . they are bent eagerly on wrongdoing, the officer, . . . the judge, . . . the nobleman, . . . thus their goodness is twisted like rank weeds, and their honesty like briars. . . . Trust no neighbor, put no confidence in your closest friend; seal your lips even from the wife of your bosom." This grim picture reveals the total breakdown of believability and stands as a warning for any people who have begun to slide in that direction. But notice that the prophet refuses to accept this situation as final and hopeless. He points again in the one direction from which a cleaning and renewal can come. "I will look for the Lord, I will wait for God my saviour; my God will hear me." And through the darkness he glimpses again the light of the utterly reliable and believable God. "O my enemies, do not exult over me; I have fallen, but shall rise again; though I dwell in darkness, the Lord is my light."

What is it that makes a man, or a God, believable? First, there is the quality of what we call integrity. It is a word that we use to describe men and women we have known or have read about, whose lives have a rocklike quality on which we can depend. Its literal meaning is wholeness, soundness, being complete and undivided. The believable man or woman is one who has achieved a degree of unity of character so that we never find him or her wavering, however circumstances may change. The unbelievable character, on the other hand, is one who seems to have no fixed point of reference. He is one kind of person at home, another in business, and yet another in church.

This wholeness and unity means, among other things, that there is a real correspondence between word and action. There is the smallest possible gap between promise and performance. We have known people of whom we could say, as Anthony said of Brutus:

*His life was gentle, and the elements
So mixed in him that Nature might stand up
And say to all the world, "This was a man!"*

This is the person we are ready to believe—one who has brought the elements of which he is composed into a simple unity of character and purpose, the man or woman of integrity.

Here too lies the secret of the communication of faith in the Christian God. It is not enough for the pulpit to echo the prophetic call to trust in the steadfast love of God, to receive and follow the Savior he has sent. The message is unbelievable unless there is an integrity in those who profess the Christian name, a correspondence of word and action. The most damning remark that can be made to one who proclaims the gospel is: "What you are speaks so loud I cannot hear what you are saying." That applies to everyone who has openly professed that Jesus Christ is his Lord. If we show no sign in our daily life, our behavior at home or at work, our enthusiasms, our opinions, and our idle chatter that we are motivated by Christian love, we are simply unbelievable when we join in Christian worship or commend the Christian way.

There has never been a time in recent history when the world seemed more conscious of this question of Christian believability. Not long ago I found myself often defending the believability of a Christian doctrine. Now I find that most people seem less troubled about believing certain statements of the creeds than they are about believing *us*. If we talk of Christian love but show little concern for the tragedies of war or poverty or hunger, we are not very believable. If we take solemn vows of church loyalty and then make it clear that neither attendance at worship nor financial support has any serious priority, we are not very believable. And if we profess to have confidence in the victorious love of Christ and then show ourselves more worried and timid than the agnostic next door, we are not very believable. The modern world looks for some integrity in professing Christians—and it is right to expect that.

Another quality that makes for believability is the strength of one's dedication, the length to which a man or woman will go in loyalty to convictions. There are people who impress instinctively with the depth of their convictions, while others leave the impression that if circumstances changed they might be found in another camp. If we think of some of the Christian thinkers who have made most impact on recent generations, we shall find that they were men who did not necessarily produce the most brilliant arguments but whose lives witnessed openly and unmistakably to the depth of their conviction. I think of Schweitzer, of Barth, of Bonhoeffer. Our world has found such men believable when the appeal of other brilliant exponents of the Christian faith has passed them by.

One other quality of believability is more subtle, and yet I believe it is always there. To be believable we must believe in ourselves. I am not talking about arrogant self-confidence, about the projection of our ego, but about the inner confidence that quietly accepts the value God has set upon us. From things that have been said to me by people in some kind of trouble, as well as from some knowledge of my own heart, I would say that the lack of trust and confidence in other people and in God that infects our common life is linked with a disintegration of belief in ourselves. Has any generation ever talked so much about "the problem of identity"? Can you imagine any of the great figures who have inspired trust, whether in public life, in the church, or among a circle of friends, being worried about believing in themselves? Not all, by any means, have been Christian believers, but I doubt if the right kind of self-belief can ever be generated without some conviction about a greater power who believes in us.

That leads me to the central question of our confidence in a believable God. And it leads me to the words of Paul with which I began. "I know whom I have believed." We misread the Bible if we think of it as an anthology of religious writings telling us *what* to believe. It is a living record compiled by those who knew *whom* they believed and want to introduce us to him. In the Old Testament the Lord God is not believable because someone was clever enough to prove his existence and justify his laws. He is believable as the one who led his people out of Egypt, who sustained them through trial and disaster, who revealed himself to every believer as totally and unfailingly dependable. The psalmist does not plead for an abstract belief in the sovereign mercy of God. He says: "We went through fire and through water: yet thou hast brought us forth into a spacious place."

It is because this God wants us to have this personal trust in him that his final revelation was not a definitive manual of doctrine and behavior, but a person—the most believable person who ever walked this earth. The moment came when God simply said: "This is my beloved Son: hear him."

Integrity? A total unity of word and action, or promise and performance, a fierce simplicity, and an utter singleness of mind—that is Jesus as we find him in the Gospels. It was exactly that which disturbed an anxious and unbelieving people. "The crowds were astonished at his teaching, for he taught them as one that had authority, and not as the scribes." The scribes, like us, were often living on a lower level than their words. Jesus spoke with the authority of a total integrity—and that is why "the common people heard him gladly."

Dedication? A willingness to go to the limit in pursuit of his calling, and in obedience to his

God—that is Jesus as we find him in the Gospels. This is the one who, when the hour strikes, turns his back on the welcoming crowds by the Lake of Galilee and sets his face to go to Jerusalem. Is there any greater test of believability than a willingness to die for one's beliefs? It is supremely the cross that has drawn men and women of every age to put their trust in this Son of the living God. "I, if I be lifted up, will draw all men unto me." It is this suffering and dying Christ who has made the love of God believable for millions who have been through the agonies where that love seems but a mocking word.

And then—his quiet, undemonstrative, but unswerving belief in himself. As Son of God he never for a moment loses confidence that he speaks the Father's words and does the Father's will. To hear him override even the greatest teaching of the past with the words "but I say unto you" is to be in the presence of one in whom we can confide as in no one else.

It is this Jesus in whom Paul believed. It is this Jesus who is still among us, able to create the confidence we need. For he reflects the God whom we can trust in this world and the next. And to be able to say with Paul "I know whom I have believed" is not only to have this assurance from the one who has conquered death and sin, but to be on the way to being transformed into his image, to become ourselves what this world so desperately needs—believable people.

"I'm gonna cut your ...
you're going to wat...

"He'll do it too!" someone in the crowd whispered.

But before the whispering onlooker had said three of his four words, Tallman kicked at Morton's hand and sent the knife sailing. While the stunned woman beater was looking at his empty hand, Tallman kicked the still kneeling hulk square in his jaw. A mist of blood and several teeth erupted from Morton's mouth and he fell back.

To be sure, Tallman walked forward and dug the heel of his boot into Morton's face until the thug stopped moving.

That's when he heard the hammer on a revolver . . .

"Matt Braun is one of the best!"

—Don Coldsmith, author of The Spanish Bit series

"He tells it straight—and he tells it well."

—Jory Sherman, author of *Grass Kingdom*

"Braun blends historical fact and ingenious fiction . . . A top-drawer Western novelist!"

—Robert L. Gale, Western Biographer